HARRIS HAWK & REDTAIL HANDBOOK

Dedicated to Cliff Yarrow

He flew above Eagles

INDEX

INTRODUCTION

CHAPTER 1 - THE SPORT OF KINGS

CHAPTER 2 - IS IT FOR YOU?

CHAPTER 3 – WELCOME TO THE HARRIS HAWK

CHAPTER 4 – WELCOME TO THE REDTAIL HAWK

CHAPTER 5 – PREPARING

CHAPTER 6 – EQUIPMENT

CHAPTER 7 – FOOD

CHAPTER 8 – NEW ARRIVAL

CHAPTER 9 – MANNING

CHAPTER 10 – TRAINING & HUNTING

CHAPTER 11 – LOST BIRD

CHAPTER 12 – HEALTH AND DISEASE

CHAPTER 13 – THE FINAL WORD

INTRODUCTION

Way back in the year 1965, when Harold Wilson was prime minister of this great country (thankfully keeping us out of the Vietnam war), and winning the World Cup was just a glint in Bobby Moor's eye, I was a ten year old nipper. With a head full of broken toys, I went looking for adventure with my equally beguiling ragamuffin school pals, Barry Harwood, Paul Weston and Peter Morris. Do we ever have friends as loyal as those from our youth? Probably not. It's a different kind of friendship that blooms from the centre of your heart and lasts forever. Nothing can take away that honesty or that gullible bond of innocence. Best friends – that's a promise - not a label.

The word 'bond' will be prominent throughout the writings in this book, because the bond of companionship is a sacrifice to compromise. An alliance and worldly attachment, like those days of our youth.

***

Let me introduce you to the lovable, uncompromising, unshakeable, Charlie Sinclair. In 1965 Charlie was an elderly pigeon fancier who owned an allotment close to where I lived. He seemed 90 years of age when I was ten; and he still seemed 90 when I was thirty. An old retired miner, hardened by a lifetime of chiselling out coal from a damp, dark coal-face. Birds were his passion, as they were mine, too, and he would sit in his pigeon cree (old shed) or roam the woods and fields with his binoculars from morning until night, no matter the season or weather. He did it to: "Keep away from the wife," he would joke, but, according to my father, he probably meant it. My friends and I would see him often as we played in the local woods. Those were different times. Our mothers never feared where we were, as long as we all stuck together and we returned home for our tea. Which we always did.

This one particular day we saw Charlie by the edge of the wood scanning the horizon with his gigantic binoculars (or "bonny-pockulars" as I called them in those days) looking like a soldier on manoeuvres.

"What are you looking for, Charlie?" I asked.

He had a fringe of grey-white hair protruding from his old navy blue moth-eaten cloth cap. A face full of character that Walt Disney could have made famous.

"Have you lads seen a Kestrel flying around here?"

"Kestrel? There's a pair over Waldridge Fell," said Barry. "They nest in a conker tree close to the old pit. Tough climb, though Charlie. I wouldn't try it."

"Climb trees? How old do yer think I am, yer daft sod," he replied abruptly. "I'm looking for a Kestrel with leather straps tied to its legs."

"Who's done that to it?" Paul, the youngest of our gang, quizzed.

"It's a trained bird. The straps are called jesses."

That meant nothing to us. Nobody replied, we all just looked at each other with either a vacant expression or a shrug of the shoulders. He explained how a friend of his had lost his falconry bird and there would even be a reward should it be return it to its owner.

"What's the reward, Charlie?"

"I'll give yer all a tanner (six pence) and a Mars bar each!"

That was it – the summer holidays were sorted. What better way to spend the school break than chasing after a bird with the added impetus of a tanner and a Mars bar each as our prize? Obviously we needed equipment. You cannot catch a bird without equipment, it goes without saying.

"You will need a glove," said Charlie. "So it can land on your hand and not chew your little fingers off."

There were four of us, Barry, Paul, Peter and myself, so that meant four gloves.

"I've got a pair of goalkeeper's gloves," replied Peter.

In the world of falconry we assumed that one glove each would be enough, so we needed another pair of 'something' to equip us all. Paul's grandfather unknowingly supplied the other two … gardening gloves. That was the safety aspect sorted, and apparently we needed some string to tie up the jesses. There was always string in our house so I was happy to take that along. Off we set. Four kids; one glove each; a ball of string; four packets of crisps; two cheese sandwiches; and a packet of Jaffa cakes. We were all deadly serious about this, and that carries more possibilities in a child's mind than any of us could be conscious of. Today's modern equivalent is probably 'Game Of Thrones'.

***

We did see a Kestrel, more than once, but it was probably the male from the pair Barry mentioned earlier. After screaming at it in the hope that it would drop out of the sky and land on the gloved hand, we became equally frustrated when it showed no interest whatsoever. So we decided perhaps out tactics were wrong. Peter realised the main stumbling block: "No wonder it flies away, we don't know its name!"

How could it possibly come to us if we were shouting Brian when it was called something like … Billy?

We went to see Charlie and he informed us that, as far as he knew, the bird was just called 'Kestrel'. At least we now knew, and as Paul had been shouting 'Kestrel' for most of the afternoon, the day was not wasted.

Charlie did point out: "Lads, if it hasn't got leather on its legs, its not trained, is it? Use your noggins. You need to look for the leather. By the way, what meat did you use on the glove?"

Meat?

"What's the meat for?" asked Barry.

"That's what they eat," said Charlie. "The bird won't land on your hand just for the sake of it. Howay lads, you need to get organised."

"I knew it!" said Paul. "That's the trick – meat. I saw a film about Vikings and the bird ripped a man's eye out and ate it."

"What? A Kestrel?" asked Charlie, not convinced.

"Could have been an Eagle, Charlie. It was certainly from Viking country," added Paul.

"Where are we going to get eyeballs?" asked Barry. "From the butchers? Cow's eyeballs?"

We all fell about laughing.

"You don't need bloody eyeballs!" barked Charlie, "Any sort of meat will do."

Where could we possibly get meat from? Peter said his grandfather had thrown some bacon in the dustbin from breakfast that very morning: "But it could be covered in tomato sauce," he said rather dubiously.

"Maybe that isn't a bad thing," said Paul. "Perhaps the bird will think it is blood."

At last we were thinking 'falconry'.

***

Sadly, the bacon didn't do the trick. The Kestrels, Sparrowhawks and Buzzards we saw, never gave it a second glance. They obviously weren't falconry trained or they would have been on the glove in the blink of an eye. Or so we thought.

We never did find a bird with jesses, and (according to Charlie) neither did the falconer who lost it. But for a couple of weeks in those summer holidays of 1965, the four of us were on a quest, and I don't think any of us will never forget it. For good or bad reasons, some people never escape their childhood, and I never left mine. From that moment onwards, following on from a daft kid's adventure roaming Waldridge Fell, all I wanted was a bird of prey. Falconry seemed fun … even when some of them get away.

***

It could probably be said that this book was started (in my head) with my first connection with a falcon on the glove. It wasn't a 'falconry experience', which are offered at most bird centres these days. It was when the only falconry 'experience' available was to own your own bird.

1973 was the year, and by this time I was approaching 18 years old. Charlie turned up at our house holding a large cardboard box.

"You know you said you wanted a bird of prey?" he asked. "I've got an injured bird. Any good to you? It flew into my greenhouse half an hour ago chasing a Sparrow, then knocked itself senseless trying to find a way out. Then our neighbour's cat mauled it before it could get out the door."

I took the box into the living room and slowly opened the top. I peeped inside. Huddled on the cardboard floor, shaking like a leaf, was a dishevelled male Kestrel, looking more dead than alive. This was the first bird of prey I ever held in my hands. I carefully lifted it out of the box and examined its flight feathers. The bird was too frail and exhausted to put up a fight.

"It just needs a good rest," said Charlie. "There's a few feathers missing, but I think it's pride is hurt more than its wings. It's dazed and concussed."

I placed some chopped up beef in the box and by 8pm the next morning most of it had gone. Feeding such a wild petrified bird was a lot easier than I imagined. I'm pleased to say that the Kestrel survived and was returned to the wild (eventually). I still remember the moment Charlie and I set it free. But the time between the cat's claws … and independence ... was an incredible journey that changed the bird's life … and mine.

***

If this book inspires you to obtain a bird you will quickly understand that, regardless what scientists may say, birds do 'talk' to humans … but only to those who know how to listen.

Thank you for purchasing 'Harris Hawk & Redtail Handbook'.
Happy flying dear friends.

Kev Fletcher.

CHAPTER ONE – THE SPORT OF KINGS

Henry's White Falcon

The 'Sport of Kings' is a self-absorbed blue-blooded title that applies to thoroughbred horse racing, due to its popularity with aristocrats and royalty over the centuries. A long time ago, when King Henry VIII was marrying, devoicing and beheading, the 'Sport of Kings' meant exactly what it suggests - the sport that kings not only engaged in, but excelled at. That sport was falconry.

The expression was originally meant for hunting with hawks, championed by monarchs and sovereigns of the day. None more so than King Henry himself. Nicknamed 'Copper nose', after he issued cheap currency during the English Reformation, Henry amassed great wealth, and he was never shy financing his love of birds of prey. The Royal Falconer was treated with enormous respect and was considered fourth in line of seniority in the court. According to the old book "Hawking Or Faulconry" (Richard Blome), in 1686 the Royal Master Falconer was paid an incredible £1,372 per annum to maintain the 'royal mews', the place where the birds were trained and housed. An astonishing amount of money considering the average yearly wage for a farm worker was less than £18, and a general labour only £2 more.

History tells us that Henry was a skilled falconer, flying Goshawks, Lanners and Peregrines. However, that kudos most probably came from the king, himself. History is written by winners, and no-one did more writing (about himself) than the Tudor king. It was a brave soul who criticised Henry, because they knew they would suffer the consequences. An individual who had the power to banish the Pope and Catholicism, behead two wives, and have the ability to fly Goshawks, knows they can write their own history. His pet name for his second wife, Anne Boleyn, was 'White Falcon.' During the early romantic days of their courtship, before Anne had a date with the axeman, Henry presented her with a white Gyrfalcon on her birthday. So it is assumed that Anne, too, 'dabbled' in the sport, if only to be seen in public to show an interest.

Falconry Lost Its Prestige

The 17th century was historically known as the 'Golden Age' of falconry. However, when improvements were made to the rifle, and it was available for leisure time (as well as for war), shooting became the sport of the gentry. The reasoning was simple. Why should noblemen train, maintain and feed hawks, when pulling a trigger could get them the same results - Pheasant and rabbit for the pot? The sport was in decline.

Falconry had lost its prestige as far as royalty was concerned, and it fell out of fashion with the gentry. Efforts were made to keep it alive in the formation of the Loo Hawking Club, but that died out in 1853, to be replaced by the Old Hawking Club. That saw success in its own right, and its history is well documented in Victorian falconry books. As with everything else, time caught up with it, and in 1927 the Old Hawking Club was no more, replaced by the British Falconers' Club, which still lives on to this very day. It currently has around 900 members across 13 regional areas in the UK.

Is there still a class divide in falconry? That's a difficult one. Maybe there was social division decades ago when Peregrines and Goshawks cost as much as a family car, and only the wealthy and affluent could afford them. Not so much now in the 21st century. You don't have to be well-heeled or rich these days, because birds that are seen as being true to the sport (those that can take sizeable prey) are available at prices that are within reach of almost everyone.

Personally I have never found the need to join a guild or association, or even the British Falconers' Club, to help me fly a bird. To my mind, the remoteness is the joy. However, I also understand why enthusiasts enjoy the companionship of like-minded people.

There has long been a general code of practice amongst falconers as regards clothes and conduct, and they still do try to discourage the guys in khaki combat gear. I was invited to a field meeting once, only on condition that I didn't wear my old camouflage jacket, which I was well known locally for wearing. Apparently, it's not what you look AT that matters … it's what you SEE. Conduct is a respect for the sport that you are engaged in, and respect for yourself. I believe I have both. Perhaps it had nothing to do with class at all, but they didn't didn't like that jacket, for sure!

The general public (as a rule) love to see birds of prey. The success of falconry, owl and hawking centres proves that point. The chance to view such majestic creatures at close quarters is not something they come across every day. But it is a controlled environment run by experienced people. The public only get to see what they are shown, and many believe it is natural for those birds to act in such a social manner. The heart of falconry is the kill, and that would be very upsetting to many observers if they saw it happen right in front of their eyes. Would children ever sleep again having seen what happens to cuddly bunnies when the wolves of the sky get hold of them? We are involved in field sports, and as responsible sportsmen and sportswomen, we must understand the need for good conduct and good 'press'.

Falconry's Involvement In Field Sports

Falconry is broadly linked with the country pursuits – hunting, shooting and fishing – all tied up in one package known as 'Field Sports'. There are numerous clubs, associations and societies backing field sports in the UK, because all of them (hunting, shooting, fishing and falconry) are potential targets for government legislation. Admittedly, some are more under threat than others. I don't think falconry has a bad press at all. However, we need to keep it that way, all prim and proper, and squeaky clean.

Fox hunting continues to come under pressure from protesters, despite hunting with dogs being banned since 2004. The law requires that the fox has to be shot by hunters rather than killed by hounds. That still hasn't satisfied everyone, and many demonstrators want it banning completely. There were 192 registered hunts in the UK in 2019, with protesters at most of them. Demonstrators resolute in their conviction, unwavering in their beliefs, seeking as much media coverage as they can muster. Alternatively, the training and flying of birds of prey is very much society-friendly. The kill is not a priority. The quality of the flight is the primary issue, and nothing is stage-managed, certainly not where I am concerned. Everything we fly at has every chance of escape. We don't seem to be under threat from anyone because we do our job with compassion for the birds we fly and the quarry they chase. But, as falconers, we need as many supporters as we can get. The public know that our birds are set free and they have every opportunity to fly into the wilderness should they so desire. But they come back because they have a good life. Yes, that is how we try to promote ourselves, but more important, that is also the truth!

There are more people flying birds of prey in this country than at any time since the Tudors. The sport is accessible to the masses, and in my opinion, that can only be a good thing. It is because of falconers, conservationists and captive breeders that the Peregrine and Goshawk were saved from extinction in this country. Their future in the wild hung in the balance for decades. Not any more. Falconry is no longer the sport of Kings … but it is safe in our hands, as long as we keep it that way.

CHAPTER TWO – IS IT FOR YOU?

What Is Falconry?

This book is aimed at the apprentice, and this chapter is for those contemplating taking the plunge. In society you've got to be a beginner before you can become anything, so enjoy the ride. The question: 'Is falconry for you', is probably answered by the fact you bought this book, and I thank you deeply. I don't want to encourage anyone to obtain a hawk, any more than I don't want to discourage them. I would simply like the apprentice to understand the reality of what it takes, and for them to have the intellect to make their own decision.

Falconry is the ancient art of taking wild quarry (wild game) with a trained bird of prey. It is an art-form, without question, but it is a sport, too.

Is it possible to learn falconry from a book and be proficient at it? Anyone can read the Highway Code, but that doesn't make them a driver. Obviously you need to get 'hands on' with a hawk at some stage, but it is perfectly practical to learn the rudiments before you go any further. It can be done because I did it myself, and I know many people who have become experts in the field, but who started with a literary helping hand from Philip Glasier or Emma Ford. However, it always helps to have someone give life to the written word, to make the odd adjustment, and right a few wrongs.

The world has changed since I was a kid. Today the internet is with us, and if you need a demonstration of whatever, there is someone, somewhere, willing to take you through the falconry process step-by-step. It is hard to imagine life without the worldwide web, accessible via our PC's, iMacs, laptops, tablets and phones. There is an enormous library of information and resources at your fingertips, and I suggest you use it to your best ability. Buying equipment could not be easier. Go online and join falconry forums and chat with those asking similar questions. Ground work is not just beneficial, it is crucial, to both the scholar and to the bird. However, the internet is not perfect. Not every source is reliable and trustworthy, and there are always those spreading negative messages. But it is fair to say that through education and experience we as a community are gradually becoming a lot more savvier.

I talk about the United States a lot in this book, because that is where the Harris Hawk and the Redtail originate (as well as other places of course). But also because falconry is as popular over the pond as it is here, and we can learn a lot from the Americans. Neither the Americans nor the British invented the sport, that honour goes to the far east, but we are up there with the best of them in training and conservation. American laws are different to ours. A novice must obtain a license, then get him/herself a 'mentor/sponsor' to teach them the ropes. That is not a bad thing, and the government should consider it here in the UK. Having an experienced watchful eye looking over your shoulder can only be advantageous and encouraging.

When you learn the ropes you will find that nothing is definitive in falconry. Every person has an opinion. If it works for you ... then it works! There is more than one way to train a hawk and there is no harm in being offered all of the options. Mistakes do happen, but if you happen to make one there are three things you should always do:

1) Admit to it
2) Learn from it
3) Never repeat it.

During the course of writing this book I refer to the bird being trained by the beginner as 'she', for no other reason than it lies better with me than constantly referring to the bird as 'it'. Learning the terminology is a big way of gaining respect in this sport. You need to grasp it, even though half of it is probably out-dated and irrelevant. Others may think otherwise. So, for the record - 'falconers' fly falcons; and 'austringers' (or hawkers) fly hawks. But, for this publication I will use the word 'falconry' as a general term, because it gets complicated with Harris Hawks and Redtail Hawks, because neither are hawks at all! I will explain later.

I held a number of polls (on falconry websites) asking experienced hawkers their view on various subjects. I needed more than 50 falconers to participate for it to be a legitimate poll. Thankfully I wasn't short of partakers, and that turned out to be a serious amount of knowledge to feed from. Their experiences can become our knowledge.

The first question was: "What do you consider to be the most enjoyable aspect of falconry?"

The top ten:

1) The bond with the bird	37%
2) The flight at quarry	27%
3) Manning	16%
4) Achievement of training	15%
5) Escapism/countryside	11%
6) The kill	10%
7) Bond of bird/dog	8%
8) Camaraderie with friends who have birds	6%
9) Getting home with bird after a day hunting	4%
10) Every day is different	2%

We can prove (or disprove) anything with statistics, and they perform an important role in today's society. From those that cast a vote only 10% said the kill was the thrill, and I was a little surprised it was that high. The bond with the bird came out top, and experiencing that connection is at the heart of what we do.

What Is Your Motivation To Own A Bird?

Not all birds of prey are suitable for falconry purposes, and the same can be said about some of the enthusiasts who want to get involved. There are people who would love to have a trained hawk sit on their fist. But that can be done quite easily on a 'hawk walk', aided by reliable and experienced falconers at bird centres.

Consider what you want out of the sport, as well as how much you are prepared put in. Time and patience are the foundation of what you can achieve. Raptors are not pets, and unlike cats and dogs, they are not social creatures. Birds can be trained, but don't expect much show of affection in return. A dog can virtually tell you its needs – a bird cannot, and won't.

It takes a lot of self-control and self-discipline to get inside the mind of a hawk. In hunting conditions a raptor can bond with its owner, but to get to that level takes a tremendous amount of manning. 'Manning' is (for want of better words) conditioning your bird to a human level. The bird sees life in an entirely different sphere to us. So you aim for a common ground, in a battle of give-and-take, than neither really wins. Be happy with a stalemate.

How Much Of A Garden Do You Have?

A lot of people fly the right bird in the wrong place. Or I could turn that on its head and say, the wrong bird in the right place. Yet it is usually too late before they realise, and some don't realise at all.

The area where you live very much dictates the type of bird you should choose. Do you have a garden big enough, and one that is secure? Children are inquisitively attracted to the unusual, and can be a danger to themselves if there is easy access to an aviary or a mews (housing for a hawk). No-one should underestimate what could happen if little fingers were poked through holes in wire fencing.

Security is always a big factor. I would advise fitting CCTV - for what it is - and as a deterrent. Cameras are the best way of dissuading the law breakers. Raptors are stolen quite frequently by opportunists, and by those stealing to order. There is a sell-on value in just about anything these days, and it doesn't take an accountant to work out that a big exotic bird can bring in big bucks if sold to the right person.

Birds are close-rung for a reason, to identify who owns what. But that isn't much of an obstacle to discourage the hard-core thief when money is available. I have seen experienced falconers take a stolen bird at a cut price if the 'lorry' it fell off was a long distance away from the home they are going to house it. Of course they should know better, all of them DO know better, but it doesn't stop them. The fact that falconry is such an isolated leisure pursuit, with most people doing it alone, they know they stand a hell of a good chance of get away with it.

What Type Of Land Do You Have Available?

Don't shoot the messenger, but if you live in the heart of a town or city, maybe you should reconsider getting a hawk at all.

A bird needs to be flown, and although every city has its green belt (parks and commons), is that the place to exercise a hawk? I live in the countryside and now and again I have found it difficult finding land that is dog-free. 6.7 million households in the UK own a dog, nine million dogs in total, and such creatures have to be 'emptied' twice a day. Dog walkers are everywhere, and in the city they head to the nearest green pasture. They probably have more right to be in a park than a bird enthusiast with a hawk, so it is always advisable to contact the local authority for permission to fly a bird on any public land. In modern society, dogs are top of the tree when it comes to animal popularity. Having one 'attacked' by a large bird of prey, in a public place, is not really a good start to a falconry career. If it happens the word will soon spread amongst dog owners, believe me.

A fellow falconer, Phil Wood, has a theory about birds and dogs: "Dogs look up at us; cats look down on us; but your bird will always treat you as an equal." I couldn't have put it better.

Is It For You?

Keeping a pet alive is a fairly simple procedure. Feed it; make sure it has plenty shade and water on hot days; keep it safe and secure.
Are you up to it?

1) Can you devote enough time?
2) Can you afford the food, shelter and equipment?
3) Who will look after the bird when you are away?

If you can put a 'tick' to each of those, maybe you are ready to start looking for a bird.

A quote in the 15th century book 'Boke of St Albans' lists who, in the ranks of mediaeval society, had the right to fly what. The list included an Eagle for an emperor; Gyrfalcon for a king; a Merlin for a lady; right down the social scale to the bottom rung of the ladder - a Kestrel for a knave.

Was that list ever upheld in a court of law? Did anyone ever lose their head because they were caught with a Sparrowhawk rather than a Kestrel? I honestly don't know. Incidentally, the Barry Hines book/film "Kes', the story of a tormented working class boy who takes up falconry, was originally called 'A Kestrel For A Knave', taken from that very list.

The Choice

Although this book is relative to the management of the Harris Hawk and the Redtail, maybe there are other birds of prey out there that you may consider. I won't go into too much detail because (although I am not biased) I don't think anything else is more suitable to a novice than one of those two birds. I will simply give a general outline of what is available in this country, and their value to the beginner.

There are three categories of birds used in falconry: longwings (falcons); shortwings (hawks); and broadwings (buzzards and eagles).

Longwings are the true falcons. The ones generally used in UK falconry today are the small British birds, the Kestrel and Merlin; and the larger Lanner, Lugger, Peregrine, Gyrfalcon, Saker and Prairie Falcon. As well as a whole host of hybrids, bred for reasons I can never understand. What can a Peregrine/Lugger do that a plain simple Peregrine cannot? There is a huge market in hybrid birds so it is seen as acceptable and right. Each to their own.

The true falcons have pointed wings, a comparatively short tail to the hawk, and dark eyes. They prefer to take their quarry in flight, so to fly these birds successfully they require open land … and a hell of a lot of it! I don't mean something the size a football field. I mean tree-less grassland measured in square miles rather than square yards.

Although the large falcons are no more difficult to 'man' than the Harris, the familiarity ends there. I wouldn't recommend any large falcon as a first bird, simply because of the way they hunt. As you cast your bird off into the heavens, you need to be at the top of your game to be in control. All manner of falcons are flown to the lure (to an incredibly high standard) at falconry centres. But the majority of those birds never see life beyond those boundaries. They are flown by experienced people who know the sport, but (like so many of us) they don't have 15 square mile of open land to hunt. Would you be happy with a routine of swinging a lure each and every day, or out flying at quarry? Falcons, more so than any other bird on this planet, need the sky.

Shortwings are described as having rounded ends to their wings. Hawks prefer wooded areas with plenty of cover. They have long tails to manoeuvre in tight areas between branches of trees, and they tackle their quarry on the ground.

I would no sooner recommend a true hawk to a beginner as I would endorse a learner driver to buy a Ferrari. The Goshawk and Sparrowhawk are out on a limb when it comes to difficult birds to train. They are very highly strung and need expert handling. Although some books claim that Goshawks take fits and die, I have never experienced that myself. They are incredible killing machines like no other bird in this country. Having owned quite a few of them, I can honestly say that I don't think any other bird of prey gets more pleasure from killing than a Gos. You can look them straight in the eyes, and only God knows what lies behind them.

The Sparrowhawk is simply a Gos in miniature, but possibly even more difficult to handle because half an ounce in weight could mean the difference between life and death. Beginner's birds? I don't think anything else needs to be said about those two.

Broadwings are Buzzards and Eagles. They prefer countryside which is not too enclosed, and Eagles need hill country to get lift from the thermals.

Broadwings are the most confusing of the three, not because of the birds themselves, because of American terminology. The three (that the North Americans call) hawks - Harris Hawk, Redtail Hawk and Ferruginous Hawk - are not hawks at all. They are Buzzards, part of the *buteo* family. Buzzards are considered to be good for the beginner because of their large size and robustness, with large body reserves to survive a drastic weight loss. More 'forgiving' than most when mistakes are made.

Although the Common Buzzard is still, to this day, valued as a first bird, I cannot see what it gives us that a Harris doesn't. The Buzzard is a bird that will try to get through life by making the least effort. They are easy enough to 'man', but they are difficult to 'enter' at game because they simply cannot be bothered. Some say they aren't lazy, they just aren't too bright. Rubbish, they are as intelligent as any other bird of prey. They just know what they can get away with. They have small feet comparable to their size, and don't have the grip of others in the Buzzard family. So they are choosy what they fly at.

As for the Eagles, without question, leave them to the experts.

After examining the contenders, what is the ideal beginners bird? The Kestrel and Common Buzzard have long been the main choice because they have always been so easily to obtain. The big shift appeared during the 1980s. A new generation of scholars wanted the 'real deal', and that meant rabbits in the bag ... all within five minutes of getting a bird on the glove. The new kid on the block, the Harris Hawk, became the must-have item. It's reputation came before it, and I remember a falconer telling me: "The new breed of wanna-be's think the Harris is so easy. All you have to do is buy a bird, throw a couple of falconry books into the mews, and off you go hunting!"

The Harris has been on these shores for some time, although it hardly got a mention in the highly respected books of the 60s and 70s. Philip Glasier, probably the most acclaimed falconer of his generation, only gave it a brief description in his book 'Falconry and Hawking', and that was published in 1978. It wasn't until 1982 that I actually saw one for the first time. Today the species is easily the most popular bird in falconry in the UK.

I started with a Kestrel and, to be honest, I enjoyed every second of the experience. It wasn't a bird I could go hunting with, because the bird isn't capable of taking anything other than bugs or mice. Yes, they will take the odd small bird in the wild, but rarely does it happen from the glove. The main problem is its small size. Weighing only 8oz, there isn't much leeway before things can go wrong. However, my first two birds were both Kestrels, and I must admit, keeping them alive was never a problem to me. If only common sense was more common, and people knew their birds' needs. They are charming birds, and I'd happily recommend them. But many apprentices want bigger birds, and that brings with it the big difference between the Kestrel and Harris. The Harris and Common Buzzard can be 'foot happy' in early training, and if one of them lashes out with its feet you unequivocally know about it. They grab, stick their talons into flesh ... and lock! When it occurs, and it happens to all falconers (novice or old school) at some stage, you will probably have a sleepless night because of the pain. I don't know the name of the medical condition, but the pain shoots up the nervous system through the arm. The added unpleasantness is that it can, and often does, cause infection. You won't get that from a little Kestrel.

Falconry And The Law

There is no law stopping anyone (experienced falconer or novice) from buying a bird of prey in the UK. The Wildlife and Countryside Act of 1981 protects our own indigenous birds, and all British birds must be rung with a closed ring and registered with the Department of Environment.

Those birds listed under section 7, schedule 4 are: Golden Eagle, Osprey, White Tailed Eagle, Goshawk, Marsh Harrier, Montagu's Harrier, Red Kite, Honey Buzzard, Peregrine and Merlin.

Foreign birds, such as the Harris Hawk and Redtail, don't need paperwork.

However, although the birds don't need a licence, there is a licence to 'kill wild birds in the course of falconry'. Which is birds other than crows, pigeons, and others generally seen as pests.

The address to apply:

Wildlife Licensing, Natural England, Horizon House, Deanery Road, Bristol, BS1 5AH

The government of the United States takes falconry very seriously. The sport is massive in North America, and of the 50 states, only Hawaii doesn't allow captive birds of prey. Elsewhere you must have a Federal and State falconry license, provided by the State Game and Fish department.

Getting the license is not easy. First you take a written test on biology, training and veterinary aspect of raptors. To pass you must score 80% minimum. Next you need a sponsor to train you. He/she must have a general or master falconry permit, and sponsor your two year apprenticeship. Then you must build (or buy) a suitable facility to house the bird, then obtain the necessary equipment. That is inspected by the State Game and Fish department. After paying the state fee you become a licensed falconer and you are allowed to trap a Redtail from the wild.

Training a wild caught raptor is an achievement. You forge a relationship that is extraordinary and the thought that always lingers in your mind is the possibility that the bird will rediscover the strength of its heart. That's not to say they always do.

CHAPTER THREE – WELCOME TO THE HARRIS HAWK

History

The Harris Hawk was originally called the 'Bay-Winged Hawk' until American artist John James Audubon renamed it in 1826. Having failed in the States to find a publisher for his incredible drawings of birds, he sailed to Liverpool from New Orleans, and struck lucky and got himself a book deal.

It is claimed that Audubon discovered the bird, which I find difficult to believe. According to the geological time chart *'parabuteo' (Harris Hawk)* is from the 'Quaternary' period, meaning the species is at least 15 thousand years old, even possibly a million years old. If it was only discovered 200 years ago, that would suggest Audubon was the man who named it the Bay-Winged Hawk. Apparently not. He named it Harris because he wanted to honour his good friend American naturalist Edward Harris. Some historians claim Harris was there at the time of the discovery, while others dispute it. The only fact that has any concrete evidence is that the name came about during the printing of Audubon's artwork. The bird has been the Harris Hawk ever since, on both sides of the Atlantic.

Location

The Harris Hawk is found from the south of the United States (Arizona and south California); through Mexico and Central America; into Chile, Argentina and Brazil. There is a subspecies from Peru that is the smallest of the family and its hunting technique has been described as being like a small Goshawk. Apparently, it has more aggression than what you would expect from a Harris, and is quicker on the wing. But, like the Goshawk, it is moody and (for a Harris) more difficult to man.

Peruvian birds are already found in falconry circles in this country and breeding with great success. So, obtaining a Harris isn't as clean cut as it seems. There are various sub-species.

General

Wild Harris Hawks eat cottentails, wood rats, gophers, lizards, small snakes, and a variety of birds including Heron and Duck.

They cross paths with the Redtail in the south-west of the US, and both the Redtail and Ferruginous are said to give this aggressive smaller hawk a wide birth. I understand why. I had two unrelated female Harris Hawks in weatherings in my garden. One was a year old, the other four. I had a young male Ferrugenous in another weathering and I could see the two Harris Hawks continually bullying him. When I went to pick up one of the Harris's, the other didn't mind, but should I pick up the Ferrugenous, all hell would break lose. They really had a problem with that bird. Yet there was no dispute when I picked up the female Redtail. The garden was all peace and happiness, as though the Harris and the Red had a sort of mutual respect.

The Ferruginous may not be a threat to them in the wild, but the coyote and bobcat certainly are, and the Great Horned Owl has been known to get the better of it, too.

The Harris can nest as low as 8ft on the top of yuca and cactus plants, building a nest of sticks, weeds, grass, bark, elm shoots and moss. Three or four eggs are laid, which are a dull white and usually unmarked. Incubation starts with the first egg and lasts 35 days, so the chicks are at various stages as they grow They are vulnerable, particularly from the opportunist bobcat which is known to plunder both eggs and chicks.

The young birds are brown the first year and grow darker after the first moult. They stand 18" to 25" tall, and have a wingspan of 40" to 47".

True Buteo?

The Latin name is *Parabuteo* which puts it into a family all of its own. *Para* is Greek for 'near' or 'like' – *buteo* is Buzzard. So the translation is: 'Like a Buzzard', but not enough Buzzard to be the finished article. However, in recent years falconer's escapes have bred with Common Buzzards in the UK. So perhaps the species is a lot more *buteo* than scientists originally thought.

Although the Harris is not officially a British bird, it is recognised in Wikipedia as breeding in Great Britain and Western Europe, on the strength of falconer's escapes. According to a publication by the British Trust for

Ornithology (BTO), they too accept that Harris Hawks are out in the wild and are rearing young. Their study showed 59 sightings across the country from central Scotland to the south coast of England, and in 2008 two pair bred in north-west England producing eggs. They were taken under Natural England licence and hatched in captivity. The birds, on both occasions, used an old Magpie nest.

However in 2010 and 2011 it was found that the Harris was cross-breeding with Common Buzzards in Devon and Yorkshire and producing young. There were further nests in Derbyshire and Kent, but no young.

Intelligence

In a falconry environment the Harris is full of character and no two are alike. Flying them in a cast of two females, one of them always tries to be the dominant figure. There seems a need, and an acceptance, to have a leader.

Manning is one of the most pleasurable parts of falconry, and the Harris is a joy. They are willing to learn, unlike the Goshawk that puts you on a collision course before you even get it on the glove. The Harris has a natural curious manner, enjoys the company of humans, and they love attention.

Although Black Kites flock together in great numbers, the Harris is the only raptor that hunts with the ability to co-ordinate as a group. Kites (like Starlings) have a mob demeanour of every-bird-for-himself attitude. They don't employ tactics like the Harris, that work as a team, and show a dependency (or ability) to work together to get quarry. That make it an incredibly intelligent bird in the family of avian predators.

They are very territorial, hunt in packs and work to various strategies, so they are constantly communicating. They may send one of their number to tackle prey, and have five or six in tactical positions blocking all escape routes, or decide to dive-bomb one after the other. They don't stick to one plan, they do vary it, and they have more than three ways of attack. That is a very complicated operation for an assemble of birds. The high intelligent end of the animal kingdom – the big cats, hyenas, dolphins and killer whales – can work to a strategy, too. But they are mammals that are accepted as being exceptionally clever. So, in essence, never underestimate the brain power of a Harris.

Success Story

Harris Hawks are a huge success story. They breed readily in captivity, so that makes them inexpensive to buy. A friend of mine who breeds the species said: "I'm not pairing them up this season because it's difficult to get genuine buyers. Harris Hawks attract the wrong type of people because they are very accessible and cheap. The genuine falconry guys go for Goshawks and Peregrines."

I struggle with that because you cannot pigeon-hole people on the strength of the birds they buy. I know individuals who are "genuine" guys, but have bought Goshawks when maybe they should have saved some of their brass and gone for a cut-price Harris. One friend paid £800 for a Finnish Goshawk, took it to Kielder Forest for its very first free flight, and he never saw it again!

There are websites for people who report lost birds of prey, and the number of Harris Hawks outnumber any other species by some degree. However, if the Harris is the most popular bird numerically, common sense suggests there will be more of them lost than any other bird. That's common sense. Those figures usually show missing birds whose owners are desperate to find them, but those owners don't always log back in to say they have found what they were looking for. Anyone can lose a bird for a whole host of reasons, but I'm sure the vast majority of falconers get their birds back.

Harris Hawks And Dogs

Even though many falconers hold the Harris in high regard, my friend Brian Russell commented: "They are the best and worst thing that has happened to British falconry. The Harris is changing. When they first became popular in the UK they had an instinctive fear of dogs, because the coyote is its natural enemy. But I've seen Harris Hawks attack dogs with a ferocity that I've only ever see from a Golden Eagle, and Eagles are many times the weight of a Harris."

Is it possible that captive breeding in the UK for 40 years has changed the character and actual nature of the species to that extent?

I must admit, I have witnessed a Harris attack a spaniel. The bird had a Pheasant pinned down next to fence and the spaniel appeared out of nowhere (on private land) and tried to take its kill. The dog received a foot in the face for its troubles, and the bird's talons had to be prized out of its jaw. However, I have seen a Goshawk do the same, so it's not unique to the Harris.

I held a poll and asked Harris owners if they had experienced their bird attacking a dog. I was staggered when 72% replied saying they had. That statistic is not going to win any popularity vote with dog owners.

They can be aggressive but very often they get wrongly identified. I saw a report in a Derbyshire newspaper about "an escaped Harris Hawk" that was terrorising people in a local park. A gentleman (who was attacked) had two gashes across his scalp, and he had the photographic evidence. But the strike was made at night. A Harris at night? The incident happened in Chellaston, a suburb of Derby: "I recall hearing what I now know was the bird's wings flapping behind my head, but other than that, there was no warning. It was obviously trying to pick me up or land on me."

Trying to "pick me up"? A Harris Hawk? It turned out to be a Tawny Owl protecting its nest, not a man-eating Harris or Harpy Eagle. I suppose adding a hawk to the story made it more interesting. You know the slogan for newspaper reporters: "Never let the truth get in the way of a good story."

Beginners Bird

Those falconers (and I know many of them) who say the Harris presents "nothing in the way of a challenge" are entitled to their own opinion. From the other side of the fence is the guy who told me the bird "doesn't get enough credit". I had a long discussion with him on social media, and he said it was "disrespectful" to call the Harris a beginner's bird because: "It is everything a falconer could want".

I agree with him - it is everything a falconer could want - but it is still the perfect bird for the novice. There is no mistaking the fact that Harris Hawks are remarkably intelligent, and although that intelligence makes the bird easier to train, it depends on the intelligence of who is doing the training for it to be successful.

CHAPTER FOUR – WELCOME TO THE REDTAIL

Eagle Feather Law

In the States the general public refer to the Redtail as a hawk, but American law regards it as an eagle. Both are wrong. It is not a true *accipiter* like the Goshawk, and although it maybe a distant cousin to the Golden Eagle, it's not close enough to take the family name. However, in America, they regard Buzzards as Vultures, but that is another story.

No-one can underestimate the importance of the Redtail in American culture. It's feathers, like those of the Golden Eagle and Bald Eagle, are considered sacred by the American indigenous people and are used in religious ceremonies. They have adorned the regalia of native Americans for centuries and are covered under the current constitution of the 'Eagle Feather Law'. American Indian ancestry 'enrolled in a federally recognized tribe' are legally authorized to obtain Eagle (including Redtail) feathers. Unauthorized persons found with feathers in their possession can be fined up to $250,000. A quarter of a million dollars!

Habitat

It is generally accepted that mankind first appeared on this Earth about seven million years ago. Yet raptor experts Mary Louis Grossman and John Hamlet believe the *buteo* family (which includes the Redtail) could come from the

'Oligocene' period in history, placing it almost 30 million years BEFORE man. Buzzards being the first recognized birds of prey as we know them today.

The bird's habitat ranges from Alaska and Canada in the north, to Panama and the West Indies in the south. But the change in appearance can be so dramatic they hardly look part of the same family. There are 14 sub-species, some nearly all white, some nearly all black, with many shades of colour in between. The most northern of the sub-species (that is found in Alaska and north-west Canada), the Harlan's Hawk, is regarded locally as a breed all of its own and not a Redtail at all.

Generally there a three main phases of Redtail:
1) Yukon to southern California – the light phase with a brown (rather than red) barred tail.
2) Mexico and Caribbean – the red phase, dark brown above, amber below.
3) Canada through the central plains to Texas and Oklahoma – dark phase, above and below, and more cinnamon coloured.

The Redtail is legally protected by the Migratory Bird Treaty Act, but as mentioned earlier, licences are given out annually for young birds to be taken for falconry.

They are larger than the Harris, males as big as 18" to 24" and females 19" to 26", and the wingspan of the female can be as wide as 4' 10".

They are happy to live alongside man in large towns and are very much similar in habit and mannerism to our Common Buzzard. Both are noted for their marvellous soaring ability while prospecting for prey, or just riding the thermals just for the sheer pleasure of it. Both have been seen to hover (like a Kestrel) on the windward side of a mountain ridge, with outspread wings and tail, hanging suspended.

In the breeding season the display moves up a notch when a pair will provide a flying display of circling each other, cartwheeling and interlocking talons.

Although they spend a lot of time soaring, according to research statistics, 85% of their food is taken by perch hunting.

Food

Redtails have the predatory characteristics of large eagles, and in northern territories compete with them for snowshoe hares. But elsewhere they supplement their diet of rodents with whatever is seasonally available – grasshoppers, insect larvae, reptiles, amphibians, large and small birds, even fish and crabs. Although carrion is not assumed to be a large part of their food selection, body parts of full grown sheep, pigs, deer and even cattle, have been found in their nests. We can only presume those animals died by another means.

Although they may not have the extraordinary intellect of the Harris that hunts in packs, they do have the brain capacity to know the dangerous risks involved in tackling snakes. In a survey conducted in San Joaquin, California in 2012, Redtails successfully dispatched 225 gopher snakes and 85 rattlesnakes. They obviously targeted the non-venomous snake, because there are five times more rattlers than gophers in the area. God bless that brave Redtail that goes for the rattler and trusts in miracles.

Breeding

Their enemies are few, which is why the Redtail is so successful. Unlike the Harris, which tends to nest close to the ground, the Redtail usually chooses trees above 30ft. So the coyote and bobcat aren't as threatening. However, like the Harris, the Redtail cannot compete with the Great Horned Owl. The owl is the more powerful, even to the point they occasionally 'encourage' Redtails to vacate their nest, so the owls can move in.

The nest is nowhere near as big as an eagle's, only about a yard in diameter, but (like eagles) they can add to it year on year. They do seem to intend to keep the same partner in a sort of 'mate-for-life' sacrament. But should one disappear, or not return from migration, they can be very quick to find another partner. Time waits for no man – or bird. A male was killed in an incident recorded in Orange Country in 2013. The pair had been together five years, yet the female had another partner the next day. So, when you think your hawk is showing you emotion beyond just being the food provider, and your bond is as strong as a man and his dog … think again. Their emotion for anything, even a partnership of five years, is limited.

Redtails usually pick a tree to build their compact 'V' shaped nest with sticks and twigs, but they will choose a ledge of a cliff in mountainous regions. They prefer a nest with a view, and usually (like the UK's Common Buzzard) pick a tree on the edge of a wood. Location is paramount, even if it means moving other birds out of their nest, such as the Broad-Winged Hawk or Red-Shouldered Hawk. Although (like most raptors) they are territorial, the span of land they patrol varies dramatically on how many pairs are in the area. USA research claims that Redtails in parts of California and Puerto Rico are so numerous they have as little as half a square mile per pair to nest and hunt, yet in Ohio they have as much as 20 square miles.

Eggs, usually between one and three in number, are dull white or bluish-white, although in some southern areas they can be heavily marked with blotches of buff or reddish-brown. Incubation is about 34 days, but (for some unknown reason) usually three days longer in hot climates like the Caribbean.

Redtail With An Eagle Attitude

As with all raptors, the number of chicks that survive depends on the availability of food. There is a food chain, and the oldest and biggest always has the odds set in their favour. The last one hatched, the runt, less so. One chick, however, defied all odds at a bird sanctuary in British Colombia in June 2017 with a miraculous escape that defies belief. A male Bald Eagle robbed a Redtail family of a chick from the nest and took it back to its female partner, dropping it into its own nest as food, before heading off hunting again. It is generally accepted that birds can only count to two, and there were three eaglets already in the nest. So, by good fortune that the eagle couldn't count to four, the newcomer made itself at home. Despite being a fraction of the size of his adopted brothers and sisters, 'Spunky' (as he was nicknamed by birdwatchers) survived. A Redtail with a Bald Eagle's attitude. Now there's a thought for you. When you have courage in danger – danger is half the battle – and Spunky survived and is probably living his life from a more belligerent perspective than he should be.

Young of the Redtail leave the nest after 42-46 days and when they are about 15 weeks old they start hunting decent sized prey. They can breed at three years of age and live well into their 20's, if they are lucky. Research in the States sadly put the average age expectancy of a wild Redtail to around eight years. Of 5,195 banded wild birds, only 11 reached 20 years of age because of electrocution from power lines, shooting, collisions with motor vehicles and poisoned bait.

Eyesight

Back in the 1970's I remember reading a falconry book that claimed a falcon had eyesight 50 times better than humans; and the Peregrine could fly at a speed of over 250mph. Today science is more occupied with facts than speculation. We now know that if a Peregrine flew at 250mph its brain would explode. As for eyesight, we now understand something of what a bird can see.

We compare ourselves with other creatures because the human eyesight is what we understand. We see colours, and to our mind, what we view is the actual world. Vivid, bright, crispy clear tones of blues and reds and yellows.

Scientists claim that birds of prey can see eight times better than us, and that tends to throw some people because that seems to suggest they can see eight time further. If we stand on a hill and look as far as the eye can see, I would imagine a bird wouldn't see much further. It's the quality of sight that makes them special.

We think we can see all of the colours of the spectrum, but a bird's spectrum is larger than ours with more shades and contrasts. In a nutshell, they see colours we can't. They have four types of colour receptors … we have three. We have a spot on the back of our eyeball called the fovea that has the highest density of rods and cones. Hawks have two of them – the central and the peripheral – we only have the central. The significance is that a raptor has a wider viewing area than us, spanning a larger zone without needing to move its head. We can see 200,000 square mm; a hawk can see five times that. Plus, they can zoom in on objects because their eyes act like a telephoto lens. However, their major advantage over us is that they can see ultraviolet light. That makes their prey stand out like a beacon in a green field, because they can spot traces left by their quarry like urine and fur.

Hearing

Hearing is a raptor's second most important sense. Humans can hear a wider range of frequency but the hawk's ears are funnel-shaped to pin-point where the sound comes from. Making their auditory perception far more acute than ours. Which is why sound, more than anything else, spooks a bird to 'bate' (fly off the glove). Never raise your voice to scold or try and lecture your bird because you are wasting your time. It won't understand a word you say or what you are trying to achieve. It is sure to be terrified, putting your training into reverse gear. If you raise your voice due to frustration, I don't think you are cut out to be a falconer.

Hawks are especially sensitive to pitch, tone and rhythm changes. Recognising the different tones is essential to determine if the sound is a predator or a meal.

Every day I take my female Redtail across an old forgotten railway track heading to the woods, but at the same spot she stoops down and looks skyward. I thought maybe she was looking at Common Buzzards that circle the area, but then I realized she could hear rabbits in burrows underneath my feet. When we are out and about she does this often, always when rabbits are in the area.

In the United States, Golden Eagles, Bald Eagles and Redtails often collide with wind turbines, with catastrophic results. So the US government has tried to develop acoustic alerting technologies to deter them from entering hazardous air space. Extensive research showed that Redtails and eagles are responsive to a frequency band around four to five octaves wide. We, as humans, can hear ten octaves, but nothing particularly sensitive. A dog has our frequency band, and can hear ten more octaves higher! 20 in total.

The most sensitive frequency for a redtail is 2 kHz, which is right in the ball park for the sounds of lawn mowers and trucks, which is why they hate them so much. Their highest frequency limit is 8 kHz, which compared to humans, isn't particularly high. But what they can hear, is significantly more sensitive to what we can detect.

Flight

Birds of prey are celebrated for being fast fliers, but I'm not convinced anybody knows the true figures of what the birds are capable of. A RSPB wildlife adviser wrote an article in 2017 claiming the miles-per-hour figures are inflated: "A stooping Peregrine is undoubtedly the fastest flying bird, but the 'stoop' is gravity-assisted (more a controlled fall) and is not considered as level flight. At level flight they only reach 40 mph."

That survey only regarded flight as flapping wings, which suggests the aeroplane that takes us on our holidays is not actually flying. I can assure you, it is flying.

Their research claims the Eider Duck is the fastest British bird with a level flight of 47mph, and the Wood Pigeon is fourth at 38mph. No birds of prey were included in the Top Ten, yet the Wood Pigeon probably accounts for 90% of the Peregrine's intake of food. Those RSPB facts and figures were shot down in flames elsewhere. Wikipedia claims the Peregrine can reach speeds of 65mph horizontal, yet its bigger cousin the Gyrfalcon can beat it at 90mph. The Redtail comes in at 40mph horizontal and 120mph on a dive.

CHAPTER FIVE – PREPARING

Assuming you have decided on the bird you want, and it is a Harris Hawk or Redtail, there is a lot of preparation to be done before you make the purchase.

Falconer's Knot

The most important lesson you will master in falconry, bar none, is the falconer's knot. It ties your bird to the ring on a perch, and the technique is as old as the sport itself. Designed to tie quickly; stay secure; then be released even quicker than when it was tied. It works incredibly well, which is why centuries later we still haven't designed anything better. Even though the procedure is pretty straight forward, mistakes can be made. So it is imperative that it is done right every single time, otherwise your valuable bird will be heading skyward dangling a death-trap beneath its feet. A bird flying loose trailing a leash has just hours to live.

When I got my first bird I used to practice tying the knot every night religiously. All you need is a leash, and a ring (which you can concoct from anything you can fit a leash through) and I would sit in front of the TV fastening the knot until I could complete it in my sleep.

Most hawks will bite and tug at jesses, bells, bewits, telemetry and swivels, which is why checking equipment should be as part of daily life as weighing the bird and feeding it. However, it is the hawks that nibble away at the knot that fill me with dread. They must be watched.

The knot should be tied before you put your bird on the perch, so that means one-handed with your right hand (should you be right handed). I have given the instructions below, but I would suggest everybody learns from an experienced falconer. If you cannot find one, type 'falconers knot' into Youtube 'search' and you can adopt your very own 'friendly falconer' for the day to give you a demonstration.

1) Feed about half a leashes length through the ring then downwards, then take the tail-end left then over the top of the leash (that is tied to the swivel) back towards you.
2) Put your thumb over the top of the leash which runs upwards from the ring across the palm of your hand to the bird and hook a loop in the lower length of leash. This is forming the loop.
3) Swing the leash over the line (swivel to ring) and form a second loop that goes inside the original loop. Tighten it by pulling the new loop through and make double sure it is tight.
4) Then put the loose end through the tight loop and tighten that too.
5) Repeat what you have just done with the remainder of the loose leash for double protection.
6) To release, pull out the free end sharply and the knot will undo.

The Mews

Raptors are kept in one of two ways - they are either tethered by strips of leather (called jesses) to a perch, or they are free-lofted in an enclosure.

Tethering a bird isn't as bad as it seems, even though the falconer has to tend to the bird's every need. Some suggest a flighty bird can damage its feathers if it bates (flaps uncontrollably) when tied to a perch, but it can do even more damage battering itself about in the mews. Trust me, there are scores of ways to make sure a bird stays safe and in fine feather; and there are scores of ways the bird will try and prove you wrong. Always be vigilant because a bird can get wrapped up in its leash or tangled around something that you wouldn't imagine possible.

Top priority is to give your bird a good quality of life. They don't need much, they don't ask for anything other than food, but it is a falconer's discretion to look for warning signs how things can go wrong. Good sense and wariness can avoid all catastrophes.

The bird needs a mews and a weathering ground. Sometimes both can be accommodated in the same structure.

A mews is where the bird will be housed at night, and often during the day. Whether you want it completely enclosed, or wire fencing, is entirely up to you. Housing a bird is a daunting task because of the British weather. We don't get the extremes they face in the States annually, but it helps to build a mews as though we did. Plus, if you have a large stretch of land, use it. The bigger the building the more freedom you give the bird.

Cats can be a danger to Kestrels and other small birds of prey, but usually Harris Hawks and Redtails can take care of themselves. No matter how I try and deter cats from coming into my garden, they still appear, but they always keep their distance from the birds. I remember reading a Victorian book that claimed five Peregrines were killed by a large cat in Scotland when they were tethered to block perches. It didn't describe the cat, but to kill five in one visit, the beast must have been some size. Could it have been a Scottish wild cat, which are larger and more fierce than the domestic variety? Wild cats feed off rabbits, hares and they have been known to kill deer fawns. Or maybe it was a fox? The ferocious reputation of the fox towards all birds (domestic or otherwise) needs little explaining.

Harris Hawks originate from a hot climate, the west coast of the United States, through Mexico down the west coast of South America. So geographically, they are not suited to extended cold periods because they suffer from frostbite and blain. Some falconers take extra precautions by building a thermostatically controlled heater into the mews where the bird roosts.

Frostbite creates wet blisters on the wing tips, and if untreated, it can cause gangrene. It also effects the feet, freezing and deadening the toes, causing discolour before feeling is eventually lost. Blain is inflamed sores and blisters usually caused when the bird is caught in the rain late in the evening and freezes overnight.

I have kept Harris Hawks for decades and none have ever suffered from those ailments. Personally I think the Harris of today (in the UK) is a different bird to those imported here many years ago. Thanks to captive breeding, it is a lot more robust than many imagine. The Redtail is a tough breed, built to withstand the cold. I keep a check on the temperature in winter, and I would house the birds indoors if I thought it was necessary. But it rarely comes to that.

I build chain link enclosures with gravel on the ground. Chain link is open viewing for the birds and stimulates the brain. It also gives them fresh air and plenty of light. However, every mews needs a spot (high up) that is screened from the wind and snow, giving protection from the elements. If you build an exposed mews, it is important that the bird feels comfortable, and not battering itself against the wire.

Speaking from experience, I don't like keeping any solitary bird in a solid-walled mews for long periods with no view of the outside world. A solitary Harris Hawk needs something to invigorate it, and locking it away effects them more than any other raptor. Isolation in an enclosed mews can produce aggression towards people and dogs. The one exception is a new bird in unfamiliar surroundings. It will prefer to hide rather than be put on display. But only until it settles.

If you don't have the skill or appetite to build a wooden construction, stick your hand in your wallet and commission somebody that does. If you want the best that money can buy, an experienced joiner will be only too willing to oblige. But, unlike a garden shed, there is no a template to work from. The shape and size of what is required depends on:

1) The land available.
2) The bird's needs.
3) How attractive the land owner wants the structure to look.

I don't think anyone wants an unsightly heap of timber cluttering up their garden. Then again, the building must be more practical than decorative. It is constructed for a reason other than being a good background for the roses.

A translucent roof brings in light, but although the British climate isn't Equatorial, it can let in too much heat on a scorching day. Some go for the hybrid design for the roof - part plastic panel – part wire. That takes away the greenhouse effect that could make the bird unhealthy.

Before making a design, go visit other friendly amiable falconers to get ideas. I say "friendly" because some (and I include myself here) don't like strangers nebbing at what buildings they have; what types of birds are housed; and how secure the place is where they are kept. Don't take it personal if they don't want you there. I wouldn't either.

The overall design for free-lofting a Harris or Redtail should be 8' x 10' x 8' minimum, giving enough space to keep the bird in good feather and in healthy condition. The minimum width must be more than the wingspan of the bird, otherwise wing tips get broken.

Any windows must have vertical bamboo bars on the inside, and a safety grid on the outside, in case one of the bars breaks. Never horizontal bars or the bird will hang on and damage itself.

Perches can either run across from wall-to-wall, or be fixed on brackets. Place a perch next to the window to stop the bird trying to crash through the bars. It also gives it a view of outside. I always recommend using perches with a variety of diameters, to give the bird a choice of grip, but they love routine and usually pick one and stick with it.

Fitting electricity for lighting is an option, but indoors the battery powered LED 'push switch' lights are inexpensive and very easy to place around the walls.

You should be able to see your bird at all times, and I'd recommend putting a peep hole on the solid side of the mews. Add a thermometer, particularly in the winter. I keep daily notes on all of my birds. Log the temperature in severe weather and make notes how the birds are coping.

Another consideration is a food hatch, so another person could feed your birds in a time when you are away. They wouldn't need any hands-on experience, just the ability to pop the food through a hatch.

A popular idea from the States is to line the floor with chicken wire first, before the building is built on top. Extend it out beyond the mews walls. In this country it would stop foxes burrowing in, but they have a bigger variety of predators in the US of A. Foxes are attracted to poultry and rabbits, and many falconers breed their own bird food. Rearing quail is common, and chickens too, and that can attract unwanted visitors. I have never lost a bird to a fox, but I saw what was left of a friend's Goshawk when it was caught tethered on a bow-perch. Foxes are about, even in the most built up areas. Security lights are good, as foxes scarper the second a light comes on. Or you could install a motion activated water sprinkler close to a muse or weathering, pointing away from the bird of course.

One very good idea for a free-lofted mews is a two-door entry system. There is always the potential for the bird to fly out when the door is opened. Falcons free-lofted during the moult can be experts at this. I once saw a Peregrine cunningly beat the owner to the door, and fly out into open rolling hills just two seconds after he had turned the key in the lock. If there is no way to implement two doors, you should consider using a heavy canvas that drapes over the doorway doing the same job as a second door.

The Weathering Ground

This can be some place in the garden with a bow perch, where the bird is quiet and safe. But, if there is no roof, there must always be someone at hand to move the perch (and the bird) under cover every time the weather changes to bad. A small amount of rain never hurt any bird, and they quite enjoy it on warm days, but not during cold spells or in winter.

Some form of shelter is more practical. The bird should be able to make its own decisions, whether it wants the sun, or a chance to get out of the way of it. All you need is a wooden frame with a simple sloping roof. Or alternatively a box shape with an overhanging roof, because both the Harris and Reds are sure to try and get on top of it.

An open three sided enclosure is fine, with a wire frame as a door as the fourth side.

When choosing a perch, think of the bird's natural environment. I pick a strong tree branch and put a metal ring on it, to which I tie the bird.

The priority is to keep out bad weather, but also be sympathetic to what the bird can see. They are intelligent creatures and need brain stimulation, so try and give the bird something interesting to look at. My weathering is in the garden, that looks straight into the house through the large glass door. I can see the birds constantly as I sit in the house, and most important, they can see me. This helps with the manning and keeps the birds occupied.

Tethering a bird to a perch may seem cruel, but that is the perspective from how we see it. In the wild a bird feeds, then sits for hours until it is hungry again. Apart from the breeding season, food is everything to them. When they are fed they hardly move a muscle.

Always make sure there is something to hold the bird's attention, rather than having the poor thing sat watching next door's wall 24/7. Birds are not wired up the same as humans and they don't need much to entertain them. So, I'm not suggesting build a small version of Alton Towers, just place the perch where something could be happening.

Mews Floor

There are no hard and fast rules for flooring, it is basically what you can keep clean. The maintenance is far more significant than the flooring. Make sure all castings and discarded food are removed daily to avoid attracting bugs and disease.

Gravel works well for me. It lasts, is easy to clean with a garden-hose, and is relatively inexpensive. Dirt or grass floorings are the most natural but grass isn't easy to manage when it becomes overgrown.

Many experienced (and respected) falconers recommend sand because it is easy to rake and clean out. But I find it creates a lot of dust when it dries out. Dust can cause respiratory problems to birds, as well as humans. Plywood and chipboard are short term because they rot when wet. I don't use wood shavings, either, because they blow about in the wind and can distress the bird. Sawdust is too fine and holds moisture, while straw is organic and not recommended. Newspaper on wooden floors is never a good idea, because (like wood shavings) it blows about and startles the bird.

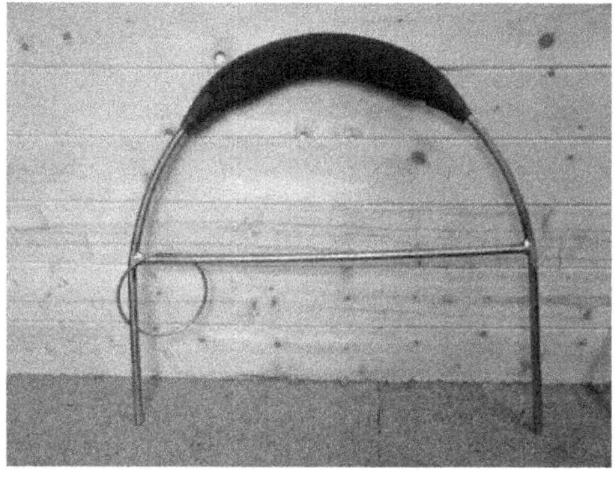

Bow Perch

Falcons use blocks to stand on, (which are a circular wooden design with a flat top) the Harris and Redtail (as well as all the hawk and buzzard family) use bow perches. These can be made, and if you happen to be a welder, you can save a fortune.

They are readily available on the internet, and there is no getting away from it, you will need one. They are nothing more than a bent metal rod with a welded angled support, and a floating metal ring. The top has a covering of rubber, plastic hose, or plastic astroturf.

Designs vary, and the type that was originally used decades ago, featured the actual branch of a tree. It comprises two iron collars on spikes, set at 45 degrees. The branch was bent, then screwed into place to join the collars together. An adjustable crossbar, with locking nuts and bolts, completed the frame. It had a floating metal ring like all other bow perches. All in all, there was enough metal in that system to rebuild the RMS Titanic! I'm sure it was an impressive piece of kit back in the 1920's, but they are rarely seen these days.

Some people use astroturf (plastic grass) on their stands, but it can be too rough for the bottom of the birds feet and can irritate them. It is used a lot on weighing scales, but not everyone agrees with it on perches.

Nylon rope is another man-made material that has a split vote with falconers. It seems easy to clean but it has been the cause of Bumblefoot because bugs can breed between the rope and the actual metal frame. The falconer is obliged to make sure everything is clean.

Most bow perches have two spikes that are driven into the soil, but another design is a weighted slab of metal on either side of the perch, to make it portable. It can be placed in the garden or on a concrete or wood floor. It is weighted so it won't topple over when the bird bates. However, they can be easily moved by female Redtails, particularly on a wooden surface. Obviously it depends on the weight of the perch, because they can vary so much. But when two or more birds are tethered in close proximity, don't use portable perches.

Ring Perch

This perch is a complete circle. The one I use has an additional metal rod that can raise it to about 6ft. My female Redtail absolutely loves it. She sits up high like Queen of the castle. The perch must have an 'X' in the middle of the circle to stop the bird trying to clamber through it. As with all equipment, if there is a chance a bird can damage itself – it invariably will.

Many falconers don't recommend the ring perch because the leash can get caught on the padding on the top. The metal ring is at the base of the pole, so this can happen if the jesses are at the back of the bird, and it should jump forward. As long as the leash is a good length there isn't a problem and it won't happen. All of my birds prefer the ring perch to the bow perch, simply because they can sit up high.

Screen Perch

The screen perch is probably the most controversial piece of equipment in falconry, to the point I am surprised anybody uses them at all. It consists of a straight piece of wood/metal, and a Hessian (or canvas) cloth hung below. The bird is tied by the leash, but it must be tied short, or bating becomes even more hazardous than the contraption itself. The idea is that, should the bird bate, it can clamber back up to the top with the help of the cloth.

The American design is metal piping, with astroturf as the binding for the perch. Imagine a bow perch in a rectangle design (24" across the perch, a drop of 18"), with the cloth tied tight across the square, on a metal stand. There you have it.

The system relies on the ability of the bird to right itself, but if a bird is out of condition or under the weather, it could end up hanging upside down and suffer a slow horrible death.

Screen perches are difficult to get hold of because so few falconers use them, but they do appear on Ebay occasionally.

Tyre Perch

As the name implies, this is made from a car (or lorry) tyre. Once cleaned of grease and oil, four holes are drilled (2" from the rim) at 12 o'clock; 3; 6; and 9. A piece of plastic-coated wire cable goes through the holes at 12 o'clock and 6, and a metal ring is placed through it before it is clamped with two U-bolts. Do the same at 3 o'clock and 9, and the ring is in the centre linked to both cables. The bird is tethered to the ring.

This is another system I wouldn't touch with a barge pole. At one point it was banned in many of the states in America (and as far as I know, probably still is). However, I know many who use them and insist: "you cannot deny they are very safe perches". They are at ground level and there is nothing for the leash to tangle around, so I have to agree (unlike the screen perch) a bird cannot come to any harm. But I don't think birds ever seem comfortable sitting on one.

I know a gentleman in the States who uses the same system with a large aeroplane tyre for his eagle to sit on. Seriously, how do you get hold of an aeroplane tyre?

Bath

Every bird should have the option of a bath, even if it doesn't use it. As well as the intake of water, bathing is very important to encourage the bird to preen and keep the feathers water proof.

Baths can be bought from falcon suppliers, and very nice they are too. However, the bird bath wasn't exactly designed by NASA, so there are other options are out there at a quarter of the price. Try your local garden centre. To suit a Harris or Redtail, you are looking for a circular plastic or fibreglass dish with a diameter of around 30" and depth of three to four inches. Large plant pot sauces are ideal.

All birds flying free in a pen should have a bath as a permanent fixture. Birds in a weathering should be offered one on a morning, not the afternoon, because they need enough time to dry out before the sun sets.

If your bird shows no interest in bathing, and you feel it should 'reconsider', put her/him on a bow perch. Place the bath close to the perch and fill it with water. Put a brick in the bath, then place a day-old-chick on top. The leash should just be long enough so the bird has to stand in the water to to get to the brick but not step onto it. If you do this a number of times, the bird gets used to splashing about and often they start to bathe.

Johnson's Anti Mite Spray

Anti mite spray can be sprayed directly onto your bird to kill external parasites such as red mite, northern mite or lice and will also help to prevent re-infestation. It can be used as an environmental spray on perches and aviary surfaces too, particularly in cracks, to control parasite populations.

It's not expensive, less than £5 for a 150ml spray can. It can be bought at most pet stores as it is also used for budgies, canaries and pigeons.

CHAPTER SIX – EQUIPMENT

How Much To Spend?

I read an article on the overall expenditure to get started in the sport, and it claims that the average novice pays in excess of one thousand pounds. I assume that price must include the bird itself. I suppose everything else depends on how much money you want to pay, or what funds you have available to you.

I worked out what I had spent on equipment and housing and suddenly one thousand pounds became a conservative estimate. I'm not suggesting falconry can be done on the cheap, because good equipment is essential, however, 'expensive' is not necessarily the 'best'.

The biggest investment is the mews, but that is determined by:

1) Can you do it yourself?
2) Who you know who can?
3) Can they do a good job?
4) How much will they charge?

Buying second-hand wood cuts the cost immeasurably. Let's not forget, a mews is a specialist design, not just a shed. It will be expensive if you pay a professional, but even if you are not a skilled joiner, maybe you could get help from friends.

The other major expenditure is telemetry, and that can cost in excess of £1,000, if you go top of the range for tablet and all the fittings. The second-hand market is the luck of the draw. You could strike lucky, alternatively you could be buying someone else's problems. It's no different to buying a second-hand car. You never really know what you are getting.

First and foremost, a bird's well-being is always paramount. It is to me, to every other falconer, and I'm sure it is to you, too. I presume we are on the same wave-length when it comes to a bird's welfare. I must point out that there are items of equipment, or 'furniture' as it is called in the sport, that don't necessarily need to be 'an arm and a leg' to do the job. For example jesses and anklets are crafted from leather, and they can easily be made at home. Even if it means buying the first selection from Ebay, and use them as a template to make your own. That way you will know the exact size for the bird you own. I know it works, because I have done it myself for years.

Glove

Traditionally, the glove has always been worn on the left hand (on the right hand if you are left-handed), and nobody has ever found reason to change it.

The glove is the most personal of all the equipment you will be buying, so maybe you want to look towards the top end of the market. I still have my first one, which is a lot older than many of the established falconers I know, and I keep it as a spare. I hate breaking in a new glove, and I admit I should have broken in a lot more than I have, but I get attached to them. They need to be strong (particularly if you are handling a Redtail) but be supple enough so you can feel the jesses and know you have hold of your bird.

It takes someone skilled in leather-work to even attempt to make one, so I would suggest you buy yours from one of the many falconry suppliers.

I know guys who prefer to change their gloves every season. That is a choice the individual makes, but it seems a bit extreme. However, if a talon goes through your glove I would suggest you get rid of it. If a talon cut through once, there is a hole, and your bird will inevitably find the same spot again.

Always keep the glove clean, even more so if you feed the bird on the fist, because dried meat can get into seams and crevices. Feeding your bird from the glove is another 'Marmite' decision you make as an individual. Some think it is the only way to train a bird – while others ridicule it. I believe in it, because it works for me. One expert wrote in their book, the reason they never feed on the fist is because: "It makes the glove dirty," and indeed it does. My advice – clean your glove – it's not that difficult.

Like falconry bags, glove designs change all the time. The new recruits are often blinded by bling, wanting to show the world they are a falconer. Some individuals want to be noticed, as if holding a bird of prey doesn't give them enough attention. They go for the brightly coloured, highly embroidered, fashion statement that frightens the crap out of the wildlife as soon as they walk into a farmer's field. If that's what you want – go for it. Life's too short to be boring, just enjoy the moment.

Short, medium or long, it depends on the size of your fist and arm, but with a female Redtail I'd always go long. The female has quite a spread when she wants to shuffle on the glove and can cause a lot of damage without meaning to. The two furnishings I would insist on is a 'D' ring to tie the leash, and a tassel which attracts the birds' eye, and also enables the glove to be hung up.

There are many treatments for leather, and it is worth preserving what you have paid good money for. There is nothing wrong with buying a glove each season if you can afford it. It makes logical sense for cleanliness and protection, because they do take a degree of violence from eight strong toes, but three years is the least I would expect from a good standard glove.

If you are going for high quality expect to pay £300. There are models one tenth of that price on Ebay that are superb, and a £30 glove will keep your hand safe, just as reliably as one £320. Amazon.co.uk have a superb selection of Starlingukpk gloves for around £30. Ask around and see what others are using.

Incidentally, I know a guy who has five falcons and has a glove for each one. He insists: "You cannot be too careful when there is the threat of transferring a foot disease."

Leather Grease

It is very important to keep jesse leather supple, because if it hardens it cracks. Gloves, too, need it because leather only stays pliant if you take care of it.

Sometimes a small tub of leather grease comes inclusive when you buy a new glove. Otherwise you will have to buy your own. Any quality leather conditioner will do for jesses and gloves, but falconry supplies often sell their own – once again, at a price. If you want a bargain you could try Effax leather grease. It comes in a 500ml jar for the same price as a 250ml jar from other makes.

Otherwise you can try the Philip Glasier "make your own" method that still has its place in my falconry set-up today. Take 1oz of bees wax; 2 and a half ounces of plain candle wax: and 10-15oz of medical parafin – melt it all together in a pan – and when it cools put it in tins. I use tobacco tins and store them. It may go a strange colour when it ages, but never under-estimate the fabulous Glasier potion. Many suppliers of leather preservative guarantee their product is animal-safe, fragrance free and dye-free. That may not be the case with Glasier's creation, because (if stored for a year or two) it can give leather a greenish tinge. But it does the job. Once leather dries, it is just about impossible to revive, and my trusty old glove had been neglected. A couple of days applying the Glasier solution and I witnessed an amazing resurrection. There was (and still is) a greenness about it, but 'imperfection creates character'. What is wrong with a green glove? They will be all the fashion one day.

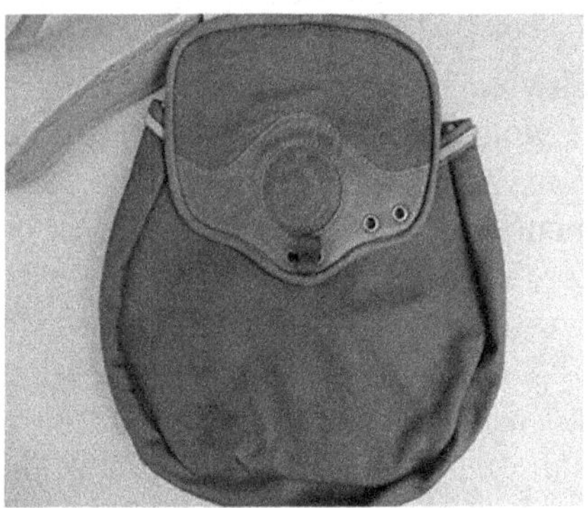

Bag

The falconry bag helps you to carry your equipment into the field and have everything close at hand. I am obviously stuck in the days of yore, because I love to see an ageing glove and a battered falconry bag. Having moved on from the traditional design, the bag can be a fashion item too. All singing-and-dancing, leather, back-pack style with logo and double straps for £250. It's a personal choice, but I think I'd rather have a Morrison's 'bag for life'. I cannot think of anything worse than a back-pack when I'm chasing a bird on a kill and I'm in need of equipment 'now'!

The vest is the modern equivalent in recent times. It is practical, with pockets in the right places and everything at hand. Some like them – some don't. I prefer the bag for numerous reasons, not least when the weather is sunny and I am down to T-shirt and shorts. I don't need a vest. But, check out Amazon.co.uk if you fancy one. They can be picked-up for under £30.

The bag is hung on the opposite side to the gloved hand, on the right for right-handed people. Traditionally a bag has at least two compartments, placed back to back so there is one either side, and the strap is located at the top (in the middle) so it is easily swung around for access to both sides. It has to be big enough to accommodate the usual furniture needed for a flight, and food has to be hidden so the bird cannot see it. Extras are little compartments for a knife, extra swivel, etc. I personalise mine with four eyelet holes for 2 mews and 2 flying jesses, which are spares and always at hand. The last thing any hawker needs is to drop a jesse in the middle of a kill in a bramble patch. You simply pull one from the outer layer of the bag, and it takes all of two seconds.

The leather design costs a fortune, is heavy to carry, and not practical for cleaning. But I do understand why people have them. A falconer loves his/her bird and devotes a lot of time to it. So, come birthdays and Christmas, what could be nicer than a leather, personalised, hand-made bag? The guy with the bird doesn't usually find out about it until the present from the partner, or a family member, is unwrapped on Christmas morning. No matter what excuse you come up with, if you want harmony in the household, you use it!

Canvas can be washed and scrubbed and is far more practical. A falconer friend told me about his modified canvas laptop computer bag that he obtained from a charity shop. That really is difficult to visualise, but when I saw it I was most impressed. It is perfect for the job. I even bought one for myself from Ebay. There are numerous compartments for a creance, lure, knife, extra jesses and swivels - plus ample space for caught quarry and food for the bird. It is easy to clean, light-weight, and everything is at hand, just as we like it.

The shoulder strap of a bag must be held against the body with a belt to keep it close to you when you run. That is why some prefer the falconry vest. No belts needed with a vest, but you cannot throw a vest over a kill when encouraging the bird that a day old chick is more nutritious and more fun to eat than the creature it is stood on. That is why a swear by the bag.

When flying your bird, take off the leash and loop it over the belt, so you know where it is when you need it in a hurry.

Binoculars

High definition lightweight binoculars are easy to obtain at a reasonable price from shops or on line. I always carry a pair in my bag (or around my neck) on every hunt, and I use them every day. I wouldn't be without them. If you want something low cost, a pair of night vision, waterproof, high quality binoculars will cost you less than £50, and are excellent for tracking game or searching for a lost bird.

Binoculars are represented by two numbers. The first number is the magnification, also referred to as the power or zoom, and the second is the lens size. 10x42 means 10x magnification and 42mm lenses.

To have a steady view using high magnification binoculars (generally above 10x), you will need to use a tripod, which is about as practical out in the field as a dog with no legs. I prefer the mini size because they are more practical if you run around a lot. Which, to my mind, is what we all should be doing.

The best, at a reasonable price of under £100, are Bresser 8x40 Hunter binoculars. Or more up-market, the Avalon 8x32 Mini HD binoculars at around £160.

Hawk Transport Box

A hawk box can be invaluable for housing a sick bird in the house over night, as well as its general use of transporting your hawk in a vehicle to the hunting ground. They are expensive, Falcon Fabrication produce them with a starting price of £150, so maybe you fancy opening the tool box (again) and making your own.

Making your own:
1) Should you decide to build one yourself, the sizes for a female Redtail are: 25" tall; 21" deep; 17" wide. Obviously is a female Redtail can fit in, so can the male, and both sexes of Harris.
2) As well as the six panels of 0.25" thick plywood – floor, roof, 3 sides and the door – you will need wooden reinforcement struts (0.5" x 0.75"); 1.25" hardwood dowel for the perch; 1" x 2.5" safety hasp; astroturf to cover the perch; handle for the roof; a lock to keep the door closed.
3) You may prefer to cover the perch with rope because some birds tend to pick at astroturf, and always check for protruding screws inside the box. Cut or file down where necessary.
4) The perch should be fitted 7" off the floor and 7" in from the door. Two 1" holes should be drilled at the top of the back panel and several smaller holes 0.375" drilled close tom the floor on the two side panels. Add newspaper to the floor (taped down with duck tape) so it is easy to clean.
5) Apply three coats of polyurethane paint, and leave to dry for two weeks before placing a bird inside, to make sure the fumes have gone.

Heat and carbon monoxide fumes are very dangerous to hawks, so air the vehicle out before putting the box inside when travelling. Avoid traffic if possible as you could find you are pulling in exhaust fumes from the car in front, and try and get from point A to point B as quickly as you can. Never ever leave the bird in the vehicle on a hot day.

*Available from Falcon Fabrication, Unit 1 Brook House Way, Brook House Ind Estate, Cheadle, Staffordshire ST10 1SR.

Scales

An accurate set of scales are significant to the well being of the hawk. Experienced falconers usually own a set of balance scales, the old type where the individual metal weights are placed on a tray. Obviously the scales are adapted to hold a perch on the other side, usually with a single support so it is easier to place the bird on the perch. You will need singular weights from 1/4oz upwards, and they can take a bird up to 8lb so they are easily compatible for a Harris or Redtail.

They sometimes turn up at car-boot sales, markets and the occasional charity shop, but falconry suppliers do sell them (Ben Long for certain). However, we are talking a three figure sum of money.

Digital scales are the cheaper alternative. They are readily available with a perch already fitted from many falconry stockists. They get a 'bad press' at times because some suggest they are not always accurate. But I think they are designed to do what they do, and I have never had a problem. However, if you don't trust your scales, replace them. Or, have two sets, and check one against the other when weighing your bird.

Whatever you decide on, never use the old-fashioned spring-loaded type that are found in some kitchens. The weight is extremely difficult to read with a bird on its perch, and if any scales are inaccurate … those are the ones.

*Balanced scales are available from Ben Long Falconry, Gloucestershire. Phone: 01452 678631

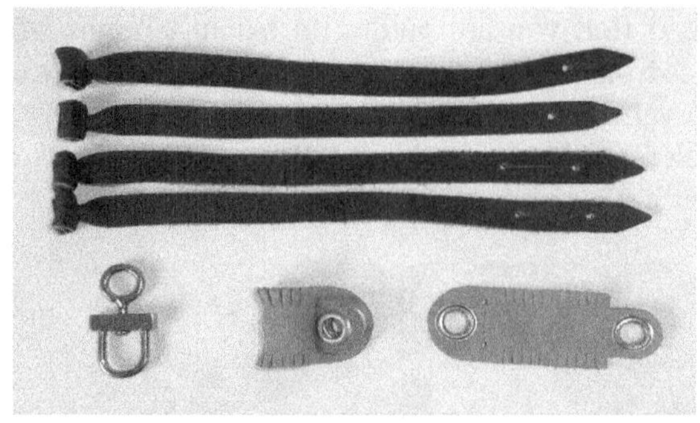

Jesses/Anklets

Jesses, as every man and his dog knows, are the leather straps that are placed around a bird's legs so the falconer can hold and restrain the hawk.

The traditional type are cut out of a single piece of leather, the wider piece folds around the bird's leg, the thinner part is what the swivel is attached to. The length varies, depending on your preference. It is very important that any closed-rings rests on the top of the jesses, otherwise (if on the bottom) it will cut into the bird's foot and cause huge discomfort.

If one historical piece of furniture has changed for the better over the years it is the jesses, thanks to a guy called Major Guy Aylmer. He came up with his idea while flying Red-Headed Merlins in the Anglo-Egyptian Sudan. The 'true' aylmeris is a leather anklet, wrapped around the bird's leg and secured with an eyelet (two rings) and sometimes a rivet. There are two halves of the eyelet and they are placed in the two holes in the anklet and clamped together with either an eyelet punch, pliers or a hammer. The rivet is placed closer to the leg than the eyelet and acts as extra security should the two rings part and the bird free itself. Obviously the anklets are put on both legs, and a 'button' jess is put through both holes. For mews or manning there is no real advantage over traditional jesses, but field jesses (jesses with no eyelets) are used when flying. They stop the bird getting caught up in a tree in branches or thorns.

Incidentally, it is illegal for a falconer to free-fly a bird of prey with mews jesses in the States. They must always be flown wearing field jesses. There is no such law in Britain, but perhaps there should be.

The 'false' aylmeris are put on the bird exactly the same way as traditional, but they already have an eyelet clamped in place. Just like the 'true' aylmeris, button jesses (mews or field) are fed through the eyelets.

Any good quality leather will do for jesses, but kangaroo skin is regarded as the best.

Braided jesses are also available, made from pre-waxed Dacron. They are strong, weather proof and rot proof, and are gaining in popularity. I have seen them in a variety of colours, perfect for the modern world and the most up-to-date and contemporary of Harris Hawks.

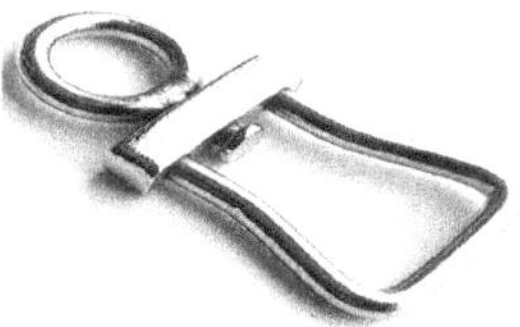

Swivel

Of all the equipment in falconry, the swivel is the least expensive, yet arguably the most important. I check the swivel every time I lift a bird, and if I have even the slightest of doubts, I replace it. It attaches the jesses to the leash and most designs are made of stainless steel. Some falconers still use brass, but it is a soft metal, and weighs heavier than stainless steel.

There are many shapes and sizes (ball-bearing; figure 8; D; triangle) but I prefer the 'D' configuration over anything else, because it couldn't be more simple to use and vet.

The one type I don't use is the ball-bearing swivel that is a type of deep-sea fishing design. I am sure they are as good as any on the market, and I have never heard of anyone complain about them, but it is impossible to examine the workings because they are hidden.

The swivel is easy to fit, simply push the jess through the 'D' and loop the slit over the swivel ring, and repeat with the other jesse.

Leash

There isn't anything technical about a leash. It fits through the eye of the swivel and allows you to hold your bird. They were made of leather in 'days of old' but everyone uses braided nylon these days. For a Harris/Redtail I would suggest buying multi-functional Polypropylene rope from a garden centre. It is sold in 30 meter lengths, either 5mm or 6mm for a Harris, up to 9mm for a female Red. Your choice.

Cut them to length, place two leather washes (obviously with a hole in the middle) through the end then tie a knot. If you like a drink, Dutch lager company Grolsch have a rubber cap on their green bottles that make great leash stops. Both ends of the rope must be burnt with a match or lighter to stop the braiding from fraying. Always make sure that when you tie the knot the rope is thick enough so it doesn't slip through the leash. Never just rely on the leash washers, the knot must take the strain. You can get a lot of leashes from 30 meters. Alternatively, certain dog leads of suitable thickness can be easier, because they already have a metal clip to fit onto the swivel. Check the clip is good quality, because some can be cheap and nasty.

Chaps

Chaps are used when hunting squirrels, simply because rodents don't play 'dead' and have a nasty habit of fighting back. Squirrels have a ferocious bite, and I have seen the mess they can make of a hawk that has lost the battle, which is why I never intentionally fly my Harris Hawks at them. You cannot always control what your bird takes a fancy to, so chaps have been designed to give protection.

They have many forms, but the general idea is a thick pair of leather ankles with metal studs. All of my Redtails are fitted with them, because the Red knows the 'squirrel game' a lot better than the Harris.

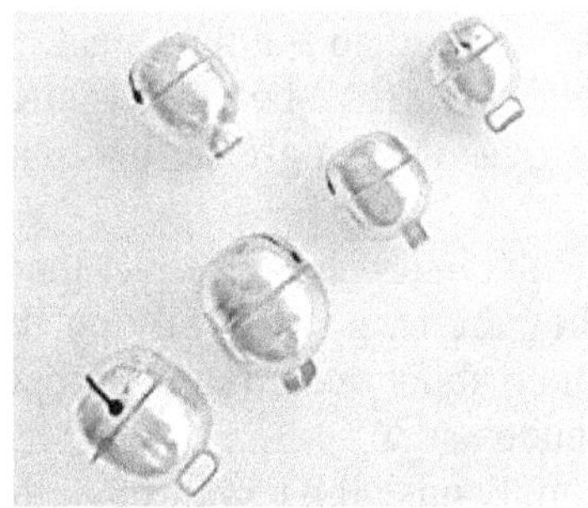

Bells

Bells are used to give the falconer an indication of where his/her bird is while hunting. There are many types and all experienced falconers have their own preference. They can be fitted on the legs or the tail. What with closed-rings, anklets, occasionally chaps, and telemetry, there is a lot going on around the legs to add bells. Most prefer the tail bell because hawks can sit in a tree and not move a muscle … apart from their tail ... which they constantly flick side to side. They do the same on quarry, too, and when a bird has killed out of sight, they will 'shake their tail feather.'

Choosing bells is a personal thing depending on your own hearing. It's a case of which pitch strikes a chord with you. I have been out in the field and struggled to hear the bells, when others close by have headed off in pursuit. But I do have a hearing problem, which explains a lot. People can be sensitive to one tone and deaf to another. Which is why I suggest you buy two different types and mix them.

The two conventional types are Lahore (mixed metals made in Pakistan) and Acorn (American double thickness), but others are also available. However, never use toy bells that are not used for falconry. You will have heard the saying "anything is better than nothing", but in this instance, it isn't.

When bells are fitted on the legs, they are tied on with little leather straps called bewits, which must be fitted above the anklets. Never use tie-straps around the legs, always leather, but you can fit the bell with a tie-strap through the eyelet of the anklet. It cannot harm the bird should it tug at it.

To attach a tail bell you will need a guitar plectrum. Punch two holes at the top of the plectrum 3/4" apart. Place a thin strip of leather through the ring of the bell then feed the two ends of the leather through the plectrum holes. The next job is to part the two centre deck feathers with a piece of card, and glue the two leather straps at the top of the feather shafts with super-glue. It's a task that needs to be right first time. Then tie waxed thread to secure the straps, but be extra careful not to damage the feathers.

There is a devise on the market that replaces the plectrum with a similar plastic design that holds the bell and has a fitted tail mount for telemetry. It is well worth checking out.

Creance

In the early stages of flying to the fist, you will use a line that is attached to the bird called a creance. Thin, strong braided nylon about 25-30 meters long, and the other end has a clip like the one used on a dog lead. Burn the ends so they don't fray, as you would with the leash.

In the past I have used a large screwdriver with a hole drilled through the plastic handle where I tie the line. I would stake it into the ground and run the line out to the bird. With experience comes knowledge, and a creance anchored to the ground is never a good idea. Should the bird fly off in a different direction, (and it happens) it could possibly come to an abrupt halt. That doesn't always happen, because dragging a line through grass does slow it down. Nevertheless, there is the possibility the bird could injure itself or, in an extreme case, dislocate a joint. It makes common sense to secure the creance to the hawking bag, which of course cushions the stop.

Dragged Creance

Similar to the normal creance. A long braided nylon line that is attached to the bird a few days before it starts to fly free and hunt. It is supposed to be a safety mechanism, giving the bird a short slip from the glove, but it rarely works that way. I think it is nothing short of a death trap. The thin line tangles easily and once a bird is cast to hunt there is no end to the possibilities. In an ideal world the bird flies low off the fist and grabs, whatever it is chasing, within twenty yards. Be that as it may, yet what usually happens (in the real world) is that the bird heads for the nearest vantage point, adjusts it two or three times, then drops. By which time it is tangled in branches and in an almighty mess.

I don't believe in them. Even using it in a wide open tree-less environment there is always the possibility the bird will rake away.

Lure

If you intend hunting for rabbits, which is usually the main quarry for both the Harris and the Red, you need a rabbit imitation. Obviously a bird imitation if you are after birds.

They are easy to make, but if you want the equivalent of the 'falconry starter kit', Ebay is probably the place to start looking. Your stuffed bunny (rabbit skin tied around a piece of padded wood) is attached by a braided nylon line to a piece of wood that acts as a sort of handle.

Magpie wings are best for a bird lure, but they are part of the crow family, so give them a good clean before putting them in your bag. Crows are notorious for things that crawl. How you get hold of the wings is left to your own discretion.

There is the misconception that feral pigeons, magpies and crows are exempt from protection. That is not the case. All wild birds are protected whilst they are actively nesting or roosting.

Some people use high quality mechanical lure machines with a remote trigger, loaded with 500 meters of 100lb line. They are usually powered by a 12v battery, with a speed control of 10-70mph. Bull X make various types with a starting price of around £800.

*BullX Professional Training. Phone: 07855227347.

Knife

In the current climate of increased terrorism and knife crime, this section is a lot more difficult to cover than it should be. A sharp lock knife has always been essential to anyone participating in field sports. Regardless what quarry you may be after, from deer to fish, a knife is generally accepted as being a tool of the 'trade' for despatching the animal and gutting it. It needn't be anything special, so long as it can be opened with one hand and does the job. But UK government legislation has strict laws on what you can carry, where and when.

The UK government website has a very clear section on knife law which states: "It is illegal to carry a knife in public **without good reason**, unless it has a folding blade with a cutting edge three inches long or less."

It is illegal to have any sharply pointed or bladed instrument (scissors, screwdrivers, Stanley knives, etc.) in your possession in a public place without good reason or lawful authority. The only exception to this is the traditional penknife with a non-locking, folding blade.

A public place is anywhere the public, has or is, permitted to have access. The land on which you hunt may, or may not, be a public place, but it is virtually certain that you travel via a public place to get there. However, as you are carrying a knife for the purpose of paunching rabbits or gutting fish, then **there is a good reason**, and you are acting entirely within the law. That covers you from travelling to, and from, the place where you hunt. There you have it in writing, now you only have to explain to the police.

Eye-Screws

I always carry strong zinc plated steel eye-screws in my falconry bag and I use them quite often. They can be screwed into a branch, fence, or tree trunk to tether a bird while out manning, training or flying. It is a lot more convenient than carrying a bow perch.

They must be good quality, with the 'eye' large enough to take the leash, and the screw long enough to make a solid hold. Always double check it is screwed in well before tying the bird.

They can be bought from any hardware store like B&Q in packs of two or 25.

Whistle

Try Amazon.co.uk for the annodised aluminium 50mm long keyring whistle that sells for less than £3. Any whistle will do, to be honest, as long as it is loud. Get your bird used to the tone, so use it every time you feed her. They are easily lost so hang it round your neck when out hunting. But if you can whistle loud, your problem is solved.

Hood

The principle behind the hood is similar to an ostrich burying its head in the sand – what you cannot see, won't harm you. It originally came from Arabia, but if Arabs couldn't afford a hood, they stitched the bird's eyes closed. The less said about that – the better.

I cannot say I use the hood often in manning because my philosophy is: "What I see, the bird sees too". But there is no getting away from the fact, it is an essential tool in falconry. It is indispensable when transporting a nervous bird in a vehicle; in the hawk box; imping; fitting new jesses; hunting; or a visit to the vets.

You can keep a bird hooded until quarry is seen, then remove it and cast the bird. This is called 'flying to the hood' and is very popular with those who fly Goshawks and Eagles. It works well with the Harris hawk and Redtail, too. Another method of entering.

Hoods are usually made of calf skin, or kangaroo hide, and the braces of leather. There used to be a small selection of four to choose from - Dutch, Arabic, Indian and Anglo-Indian - each doing the same job but with slight modifications. Today there are numerous additions, too many to list.

You can find designs on-line if you fancy making your own, and skilled individuals can do an impressive job out of a piece of calf skin. However, the proof is in the fitting. A hood needs to be a perfect fit. Placing a hood on a bird can be a daunting procedure for the novice and the bird itself, made impossible if the hood isn't quite up to standard.

Sizes vary immensely, and you don't just buy a hood for a certain species and one-size-fits-all. There are precise sizes for the Peruvian, Northern and Superior (male or female) Harris Hawks; and sizes for Eastern and Western (male or female) Redtails. Remember there are no less than 14 types of sub-species of Redtail, all different in some way.

In addition to providing your bird's sex, species and flying weight, it is helpful to the hood designer if you can provide the head measurements which are taken across the top of the head, behind the eyes.
* Contact Kevin McMillan at Hooded Talons (phone 07723442669).

Telemetry

If ever there was a revolution in falconry, it was the introduction of telemetry. Pursuing a bird was down to two human senses, the eyes and ears. Once a bird was in thick cover, listening for the bells was the only way to trace it. Now, with modern technology, it is even possible to pin-point a lost bird by a mobile phone to within five yards.

Has it changed the sport? Without doubt. It isn't foolproof, because mishaps do occasionally occur, but there is no excuse for not using it.

There are two parts to telemetry – the transmitter and the receiver. The transmitter fits onto the bird, and the receiver tracks where it is.

The transmitter, like bells, is either fitted onto the leg, or the tail of the bird. It works by the power from small watch batteries, and (along with leash, jesses and swivels) it is always wise to carry spares in the bag.

Leg mount or tail? Leg mounts are cumbersome because the bird has so much furniture around its legs, but they are very easy to fit prior to entering. The tail-mount is safer because it is less likely to come off or get caught up. The down side of the tail-mount is that a lot of birds don't like them, and some will continually bite at the feather until they actually pull the feather out. I have had this with both the Harris and Red.

The neck-mounted transmitter is with us now, used more often in the States, but I have my reservations. A short leather strap fits around the bird's neck. All well and good, but as I have said before in this guide, if there is any possibility of a bird getting tangled - it will. I have never used the neck-mounted transmitter, so maybe you should look up the guys using them for better advice.

The GPS tracker (linked to a mobile phone) is perfect. I use one on my female Redtail and I cannot praise it enough. Fully charged it lasts a minimum of five days. It is inexpensive and very reliable. I pay my phone company a small amount each month for the satellite service.

Which is best is down to personal taste. With a telemetry you point the receiver in the direction of the bird and follow the beeping sound. The GPS gives the exact spot where the bird is, either by its own atlas or Google maps.

I probably see more TinyLoc systems than any other telemetry set-up, but they are cheaper than the Marshall, which may be relevant to popularity. The TinyLoc isn't exactly pocket sized (unless you have very deep pockets) but the receiver has a fold out antenna, and fits easily into a falconry bag. I have never had any problem with mine. It is reliable, fairly compact, and easy to use. Alternatively there is the 'pistol grip' systems, of which Marshall is probably the brand leader. *Marshall of Cumbria can be contacted: phone 0161 8706518. *Falconry Electronics of Halifax: phone: 01422 376127. They always have a large selection, and they do repairs, too.

Freezer

One of the obvious necessities, but sometimes the one that gets overlooked. We all have a freezer at home, but not all family members like their frozen food sat on the shelf next to dead birds, rabbits, rats and mice. Falconers don't usually mind, it's their partners that invariably do. The only way out of this predicament is to buy a freezer that only takes (what my partner describes as): "The bird stuff!"

Raptor food is usually bought in bulk, so maybe you should consider a chest freezer. A delivery of 400 day old chicks, in one consignment, works out significantly cheaper than batches of ten.

Note Book

I would recommend you keep a diary of how your bird is developing and its well being. Make notes of food, weight, how training is progressing, flights, the bird's attitude, kill, etc. I use a large note book but a desk diary will do.

You will soon realise how important it can be. If a bird takes ill you have a record of the food it has eaten and its weight at the time. Also, it is nice to look back over a season and remember the ups and downs.

CHAPTER SEVEN – FOOD

Day Old Chicks

The idea of the bird providing for itself, with everything that it eats (killing rabbits and things that fly) is highly commendable and in the spirit of the sport. But I would recommend a good food store, just in case it doesn't happen that way.

Your new acquisition will need to be fed, and a good food supply sorted before the bird arrives. This is where making friends with local falconers can save you money. It's not one-sided either, it works both ways. I am friends with a group of guys, some I have never even met, but we all share a delivery each month that makes our 'partnership' cost effective. We phone each other, make the order, and one person does the pick-up and delivering.

Most pet shops sell raptor food, but small amounts come at a high cost. In my home village (and surrounding area) we have formed a consortium, and if we spend enough money between us with Honeybrook, we get our order with free delivery. It benefits everyone.

Food that raptors naturally take in the wild is good (rabbit, rat, squirrel, etc) if you can get it. Birds of prey eat raw meat - and a lot of the bones, fur and feathers that go with it. That roughage is very important because it all gets digested in the bird's crop and regurgitated, then regurgitated back up (not the right terminology but you will understand what I mean) in the form of a pellet or 'cast'. If I feed beef to my birds over a sustained period, I add feathers and rabbit fur to it, because roughage is significant in keeping the bird healthy.

Getting falconers to agree on anything can be a big task, and if you put two of them in a room you are sure to get three opinions. Even asking them what food to feed raptors, surely the simplest question of all, will split the vote. Feeding a bird its natural diet of rabbit and pigeon is wrong, if you listen to some people. Yet, in the wild, that is what they live on! Are we starting to pamper our birds like mollycoddled poodles?

Let's look at two sides of an argument, both on the subject of day old chicks, which (let's be honest) everybody feeds to their birds. These are genuine quotes from internet blogs:-

Day old chicks – for:-
"Birds need a good high protein diet, and far and away the best food you can give them is day-old-chicks. Hens are reared for egg-laying and the cockerels are killed with carbon dioxide as soon as they hatch out of the shell. The yolk sac provides moisture, as raptors rarely drink water, and it contains carotine that colours the bird's feet and legs a rich yellow. Chicks are generally regarded as the staple diet, but there must be other nutrition, such as beef, rabbit quail and rats."
Day old chicks – against:-

"I've heard it said often that far too many falconers and breeders rely too heavily on feeding day-old-chicks as a staple diet. Chicks are nothing more than an egg, only in a different form. High in cholestrol and phoshorus, low in calcium. Because it has just left the shell and hasn't eaten, it is woefully low in minerals and trace elements that birds get from an adult carcass."

Food – The Rundown

Unlike birds in the wild, we control what our birds eat to keep them at flying weight, so we don't allow them to have anything rich or fatty when hunting. In other words, we don't approve of them eating the "choice bits". A wild bird that catches a rabbit will break through the rib cage and eat the vital organs, flesh, bone and intestinal organs. If a trained birds catches a rabbit, we restrict what it eats so it will be able to fly the following day.

Beef is what most falconers use when flying birds because it is nutritious and easy to cut into strips that are the right size. Feeding a hawk chicks on the fist is messy, no question about it, and beef is not so bad. Both chicks and beef, weight-for-weight are the same protein. But never feed the fat – only the meat. The cholesterol level in chicks can be reduced by squeezing out the yolk sack before feeding. I don't do it myself, but some do.

It may be surprising to read that rabbit, despite it being the obvious natural food for a hawk, is low in protein and not the best diet over a prolonged period. Offer a rabbit and chick to a bird and I know which one it will choose. Never feed rabbit as the main food for more than a few days. However, squirrel is a good food, and it can be a tough challenge for the bird to get the meat off the bone. Which is good for the beak, and helps keep it strong and trim.

Rats and mice are a good addition to chicks, although they are generally given to a bird in moult or when it is low in weight and needs building up. Mice, especially, can add the weight onto a bird very quickly. But it seems they are an acquired taste because I have had many birds that needed a lot of persuading to eat them.

Pheasant, Partridge and Quail are excellent food, and Quail is readily available from suppliers. But they are rich in protein and not usually fed during the flying season. Rook is good meat but all crows are riddled with lice and mite that easily jump ship to another host. If you feed any of the crow family to your bird, de-louse your bird with Anti-mite afterwards.

Pigeon is another food that may not be what it seems. I lost an Eagle Owl to a deadly infection called frounce protozoan after it ate a wild pigeon. Frounce, as it is known in hawks, is commonly called 'canker' in the pigeon world. A yeast infection of the digestive tract (similar to thrush) uniquely transmitted from eating pigeon meat. It initially manifests itself by white spots around the mouth or crop of the infected bird. It then spreads into the eyes, throat and brain, resulting in a fatal outcome.

Duck is very fatty, but if one of my birds catches one, I always let it have a small feed. The bird needs encouragement and (in my opinion) should have a taste of what it has caught.

Although Arab falconers use mutton to feed their Sakers, mutton and pork are rarely used in the UK.

Never use road casualties unless you happen to hit the creature yourself. At least then you will know that it is fresh.

REMEMBER!

Every night you have to defrost the food for next morning. That is a simple task that must become as routine as brushing your teeth. If you forget, place the frozen food in a plastic bag and place in warm water to defrost. Never microwave!

CHAPTER EIGHT – NEW ARRIVAL

Assuming the mews is in order and all of the equipment has been purchased for the Redtail or the Harris Hawk, the next step is tracking down a bird. Hopefully you will know someone local with birds for sale, or at least know a falconer with contacts.

Getting to see the bird before purchase is a must, and obviously the more local, the less miles you will have to trek to see it. But being a novice means you need an expert's opinion, and I would always suggest taking someone who knows a good bird from a bad one. Imagine buying a car without giving it the 'once over'.

When everything is in place at home, the mews is ready and the glove is hanging on the wall, it is so easy to become desperate for the bird to arrive. I know – I've been there. It can be all too easy to get caught up in the excitement. But rushing a deal could mean you could end up with 'anything' – and you deserve a lot better than just 'anything'.

Do your homework on the seller and his history of trading. Most experienced falconers know who to recommend, but they also know who not to buy from, and that is equally important. Check the going price for the bird you are after, remembering that females are always more expensive than males. Be very wary of birds that are being sold cheap, because the seller wants a quick sale, and there must be a reason why. Yes, they could have a genuine explanation, but more often than not they are offloading a bird with problems. Beware of the danger signs.

Knowing a knowledgeable falconer has its benefits, but if you don't have that option you have two choices:

1) You either look at adverts for birds that are available.

2) You place your own advert requiring one.

'Birdtrader' is probably as good as any on the internet, but you could try Googling various falconry websites and ask who is selling.

Responding to an advert is slightly different than placing one, because the seller is usually legitimate and if anything is illegal, he is putting his reputation on the line.

If you do place an advert, prepare yourself for the wild and bizarre world of the 'internet swindler' who will try and sell you anything that he is struggling to shift. The bird world of Dell Boy and Rodney. It happens whenever an advert appears, whether you require a guitar, TV or a washing machine. Be prepared for those offloading their rubbish. The ones you need to watch out for are the people who phone offering a bird that they know little about - the ones selling for a 'friend'. There is your warning sign, as loud as a pneumatic drill. Do you trust someone you don't know? Trust takes years to build and seconds to break. I have been offered 'knocked off' birds from far and wide, some free, because the net was closing in on them.

Things you need to know about the bird:
1) It's age.
2) Past owners.
3) Is it feather perfect (if the answer is "no" ask why).
4) Hunting history.
5) It's bad habits.
6) Does it 'foot'.
7) Is it an imprint.
8) Is it vocal.

Getting answers to the questions you ask will be more important than asking nothing and listening to what the seller tries to tell you. One important tip, never make a judgement on a photograph. A photo is the image the seller wants you to see, and I have travelled far and wide to look at birds that are nothing like what is shown on the website. Having seen a photo of a female Redtail, looking elegant in summer plumage with amber chest and bright copper tail, I arrived to find the bird the guy had for sale was a male Ferrugenous with a white chest and brown tail. No disrespect to the guy from the point of the bird's condition, because it was beautiful. But, come on, it wasn't even the same species!

Damaged feathers will be put right during the moult, so if the bird has finished the hunting season perhaps there is leeway on a deal. But if the bird is a mess around September, keep away.

If possible, research the bloodlines of the bird you are after. Never assume all young birds are as good as each other, because that is not true. But it helps if you know the breeder has a solid reputation. Breeding hawks is easy enough, but breeding exceptional birds is not. It is important that the young bird is reared in a manner that it will be imprinted on its parents and unafraid of people and dogs.

Many breeders want to sell their stock as soon as possible to reduce feeding costs, because they don't have accommodation to house the chicks when they grow, and to be first on the market to get high prices.

Harris Hawks can be taken from their parents as early as eight weeks, and many are. However, they will almost certainly become screamers. They may even become imprinted on the new owner. Should that happen, when it becomes sexually mature it may even attempt to copulate with the falconer and become territorial around humans to the point of attacking them. Never accept an eight-week old bird, and always ask the date when it hatched. In the case of a Harris, no matter how desperate you are to get the bird home, never take one earlier than 12 weeks. By that time it will be far less prone to screaming and crabbing when the manning starts.

Remember that male Harris Hawks develop more quickly than females, and they are not as aggressive to humans because they are never the dominant bird in a social group.

Imprinting

Imprinting is a form of learning in which an animal gains its sense of species identification. All forms of birds do not automatically know what they are when they hatch, they visually imprint on their parents during that critical period of development.

The timing of the imprinting stage varies from species to species, but once they reach that stage, there is no going back. If a young bird imprints on humans, they will identify with humans for life. There is no reversing the process.

All young chicks are programmed to fight for survival because they have competition from others in the brood for food, so they scream at the first sight of their parents. Chicks hatch days apart and the first born usually gets the lion's share of food because it is bigger and stronger. So those further down the chain have to make their presence known. The screaming continues until they leave the nest and they venture into a life of their own, away from their food source.

In falconry terms, an imprint is easier to handle, without question. Nevertheless, if you rear your own eyass it will scream the moment it sees you, and sometimes even if it doesn't! It won't take long before the penetrating voice becomes more than just irritating, it can become unbearable - for you, your family, and your neighbours if they happen to live in close proximity. The bird doesn't grow up, and in its brain it remains a chick for the rest of its life, constantly reminding you to provide it with what it wants.

Is there a cure? Nothing that is cast iron. A change of owner and home can transform some. As long as the bird realises that the new owner is not the parent, there can be success. I took a female Harris that was allegedly a screamer and I never heard it scream once. Alternatively I took a male Harris on loan (when a friend went abroad for a spell), and it never shut up. I was sure I could rehabilitate it. I thought it was cured, only for it to scream the moment I dropped it down to flying weight. I was pleased when the six weeks were up and I handed it back! So were the neighbours.

The screaming call can drive some people to despair. During September 2019 there was a report in a Nottingham newspaper that a 27-year old father of two received an anonymous letter through the letterbox saying: "Whatever is making that noise in your garden had better stop. Last night it didn't stop until 11.30."

The falconer had taken the imprinted Harris at seven weeks old and it was a screamer. He told the newspaper: "I went to bed at 10pm on the Monday night, and woke up at 7am the following morning to see the lock was swinging on the pen. I rushed outside and saw the door had been kicked in, and opened it to find Karma still attached to her bow perch, but stone cold dead on the floor. By the looks of it she had been hit on the head with something."

There is no excuse for what happened, and the falconry community offered to raise money to fix his mews and buy him a new bird. But, like the dog that barks from morning until night, such cases can upset neighbours. I had a Harris that shrieked a mating call at day-break every morning during the breeding season that must have woken the entire street! The bible tells us to love thy neighbour and also to love our enemies, but with a screaming imprint in the garden, they can be the same people.

The exception to the 'imprinting' rule is the Sparrowhawk. Hitting a Sparrowhawk's flying weight is perilous, because you don't have much to play with when the bird is only around 8oz. So imprinting is probably the best thing to do with the bird. Even when it's vocal it isn't as ear-piecing as a falcon or hawk.

As for imprinting a Harris or Redtail? Each falconer will have their own thoughts on it, but I wouldn't take an imprint for love nor money.

The Pit Falls

You see the hawk you want and a deal is ready to be struck. If the dealer makes claims that his bird is currently flying and taking quarry, ask if you can pop along and see it in action. There shouldn't be a problem if he is telling the truth, but if he declines, maybe the bird isn't what he says it is. Falconers, like fishermen, are prone to telling 'porkies', particularly about the amount of game they take. One lie is enough to question all truths. Some people get extremely desperate to make a sale.

One young fellow told me when we were negotiating a deal: "This bird is a killer! It has killed four cats."

Why should a bird be put in a situation where it is fighting cats? Unthinkable!

If possible go to see the bird on the morning so, if you decide you want to conclude the deal, it can settle in its new housing during daylight hours when you get it home.

Never meet at a half-way point where you cannot check the bird. I once travelled 160 miles (two and half hours) to Grantham service station to buy a Goshawk for a large amount of money. I insisted on having a close look at the bird before I handed over the money, so we took it inside the service-station building. Not the ideal place, I admit, but there was space and light. I was pleased I did. It had puss-filled abscesses on the toes, pads and hocks of both feet (called bumble foot). It is usually caused by dirty perches.

I pulled out of the deal, even though I really wanted that bird. My father's advice: "The best way to avoid disappointment is not to expect anything when you arrive." But that is illogical and difficult to do. It was five hours of travelling time, and something I wouldn't have done if I wasn't expecting business to be negotiated. Everything happens for a reason – experience it and learn from it.

What To Look For

When you decide on your bird, take a hawk travelling box with you (if you have one) or a large box with a piece of carpet on the bottom to stop the bird slipping about in the vehicle on the way home. Also take duck tape to seal the box; a falconers glove to hold the bird for inspection; leash; and swivel. Ask if the bird is jessed before you arrive because some breeders don't like to hand out free furniture with a sale. Personally, if I am selling a bird I make sure it leaves me with new leather-ware, swivel and leash, knowing it left me in the best condition and 'dressed' accordingly. Others may not be as generous.

Of all the raptors bred in captivity, the Harris Hawk is the species that suffers most with congenital problems due to inbreeding. That is a variety of deformities suffered at birth.

Look at the wing movement. Ask the owner if you could see the bird flying from one perch to another to make sure both wings are functioning as they should. Take hold of the bird on the glove and encourage it to bate so you can see, at close hand, the condition of the flight feathers. Look into its eyes – an ill bird will show symptoms of lethargy and tiredness – and the eyes show a lot. Look for a liquid discharge around the eyes or surrounding feathers. Check the feet for any visual signs of swelling, scabs, cuts or lumps, and the individual toes and talons. Open the beak and examine that all is well, or does it have a sour smell. I always look at where the bird has been sitting when I arrive and check out the mutes on the floor. If it is watery and chalky with a dark fecal, there is no problem. If there is a sign of green in the mutes the bird is usually underweight, and red indicates coccidiossis and the bird should be taken to a vet.

The seller will probably have told you the bird's past history (age, hunting, etc) prior to the meeting, and the more you know, the better. But ask what food it has been feeding on.

If you are not 100% sure that the bird is healthy, either call off the transaction or ask for an eight week guarantee. You can take the bird to a vet for a check up later.

There is only one thing left ... does the bird have paperwork? Get in touch with the IBR (Independent Bird Register) and get the bird transferred in your name.

* Independent Bird Register phone number is 0161 7905613

Welcome To The Incredible World Of Falconry

You have your bird, so take the box to the mews or a room in the house and be painstakingly cautious in every move you make or your new prized possession could come to harm. Remove any expensive ornaments or knick-knacks that could get broken, close all windows and close the curtains. Birds don't understand the concept of glass. Should the bird escape when the box is opened (and such things have happened) it will head for open space, which just happens to be the window. There is a chance it could either crash into it and break its neck, or fly straight through it. Both can be avoided by simply closing the curtains.

The bird will be stressed and confused, but many falconers fit the bells during this stage (and anklets and jesses if they haven't already been put on). I'm not so sure about bells as early as this. I take them off my birds during the summer to alleviate the stress. Birds do not like bells, I can assure you.

Putting on jesses (and bells), two people are needed – one to hold the bird with its feet on a cushion; the other to fit the furniture. The helper needs to be confident he/she can do the job and not let go of the bird. They should hold the bird with both thumbs over the back, while the palms keep the wings secure into the sides. The legs held back under the tail, or between the 2nd and 3rd fingers of each hand, with the forefingers encircling the breast. At this point, when the bird is held, the other person should put a towel over the bird's head to keep it calm, or a hood if you happen to have one.

When the furniture is fitted, it is a good time to open up the wings (one at a time) and check for soiled mutes, which can be cleaned with liquid soap and water. Then spray under the wings and tail, as well as the rest of the feathers, with Johnsons Anti-mite. Making sure not to spray in the eyes of the bird, or its mouth.

Place the bird in the mews and let it settle for 10 to 14 days. Never try and drop its weight during this period. Keep it fully fed and trauma-free as best you can. It may take a couple of days before it eats, but that is normal.

Meeting The Farmer

The success of putting rabbits in the bag will depend on the quality of the land you have available to you. One of the most difficult tasks in the sport is locating fields, woods and terrain that has ample quarry.

Now is the time to start looking around and asking permission. It isn't as easy as many would imagine, as farmers and land-owners are immediately concerned about their animal welfare and people trampling over their crops. Farmers feel that if one person is seen roaming the landscape, others may feel they have the same right.

The usual downfall is if the landowner breeds Pheasants for a shoot, then you may as well head for the highway. I live in the wide open country and – on paper – the land couldn't be more rich for a falconer. I do have acres all to myself, thanks to a farmer who owns half the county, but I still have to be very careful where I tread because he makes a lot of money from shoots. However, there are benefits, because once the guns start popping, many of the Pheasants fly off in panic ... to the land I can hunt on.

A few tips that may help you get the acres you require:-

Ask permission well in advance of the season starting. Don't just turn up with a bird expecting to be given the freedom of the land. The most important thing is to make a good impression, so be polite and respectable. Show you are a responsible and trust-worthy. Don't show up in dirty clothes straight from work, because clothes can say a lot about a person. You don't want to blow it before you even make the ask.

Thank the farmer/landowner for his/her time even if the answer is "no" because a "no" today could turn into a "yes" in the future.

Have a business card with your name and contact number. Landowners like to know who is on their land and how to contact them should there be problems. Explain you will park your vehicle away from their home and won't trouble them in any way.

My friend takes his young daughter along and he says it is amazing how a well-behaved child can create a good first impression. Then if a generous farmer gives you permission, a thank you card, Christmas card and other tokens of appreciation go a long way to getting permission again.

CHAPTER NINE – MANNING

Name Association

Manning is the first part of training and refers to the bond created between the bird and its owner. I wouldn't go as far as to say it will 'make or break' the relationship, but getting it right first time is a massive bonus. The bond is a curious attachment between man and bird that is based on familiarity and the provision of food. A bird will only fly to the glove when it believes there is food there. Researchers claim a bird of prey, unlike cats and dogs, will not show its owner any affection, but, over time, that is something you may question. The connection is built on baby steps and the more time spent together, the more you reap rewards. I'm not suggesting you will get birthday cards from your bird, but you will become aware of the moment you get that connection.

What about a name? Will the bird respond to it? What name you choose is insignificant. Whether it be a character from 'Macbeth' or some Mongolian Emperor, it is irrelevant because the bird won't understand a word you are saying.

I held a poll and, 76% of the bird keepers that replied, believe their bird knows its name, or at least reacts to the sound of it. One lady put forward a compelling reason why a name is so important: "Naming your bird does matter. A bird's name is perhaps the single most important word that it will ever learn. Think of it this way, your bird lives in a sea of human sounds and, with only the language ability of a two-year old, it has to decide which words are directed at it and which are not."

We, as humans, develop a personal attachment to our names at a very early age. When a young child hears its name called, it registers a "that's me!" response. Dogs can learn that, but birds? We can't know for sure until the day we have the ability to get inside their heads. I'm not even convinced about dogs. Do they know who they are? The simplest and most likely explanation is that, over time, when they hear their name called they know that good stuff happens. Can they grasp the "I am my name" concept that we humans understand?

When I am asked my bird's name, I usually reply "the whistle", because that is what I know she responds to. I can call Khan or Maya until I am blue in the face, and get nothing back, but I get a reaction the second I whistle.

Starting The Manning Process

Getting the bird on the glove seems simple enough, and that is when your relationship starts. She has to be comfortable with you or she will bate, and that can become a daily routine. Always be confident, respect what you are dealing with, and do everything at a calm slow pace. Give warning, walk slowly towards her, and when you feel the time is right, pick up the leash in your ungloved hand and use it to transfer the jesses into your gloved hand.

Take the bird up in the fist by placing the glove behind her legs and she will step backwards when she feels the glove touch her legs. In the early stage the bird probably won't co-operate, so it takes time. When she is on the fist, wrap a turn of the leash around your little gloved finger. This acts as a security lock while you untie the bird.

Alway tie the leash to the 'D' on the glove as extra security.

That is the conventional way of lifting a bird, but some encourage the bird to step forward onto the glove. I have done this myself. All well and good, but that does not work if a bird is hooded. It instinctively wants to step back, and cannot see the glove to step forward.

Manning should be done each day, and last for whatever length it takes for you to be confident that you have achieved something. Walk around the garden at first, gradually acclimatising the bird to the sights and sounds it will face every day. Pick her up; put her back on the perch; pick her up again and walk. Importantly, get used to each other before walking out and about in country lanes, woods and fields.

You don't want to force the bird into doing things she obviously hates. If she bates to an extreme, always keep calm and never show your frustration. The bird will be able to sense your anxiety, and you ambience will change. Some birds simply don't like being carried, and you don't want her to dread the very sight of you. So use food to hold her attention. Feed her as you walk, and she will soon associate you with food, which is very much what you are trying to achieve.

This process never really stops because the bird will constantly see things it has never seen before. The difference between training a Harris and Red is the time it takes to get the same results. That implies - train a Harris in a certain time frame – double it for a Red. That is not always true, depending on the bird (some are very quick at learning), but I'd use that as a general guide. The Harris is spontaneous and constantly on the edge. I don't believe they live in the moment, it's always "what's next?". The Red is more laid back (particularly the females) because it takes more effort to move its big frame. In human terms, the Harris is more impulsive, while the Red is more paint-by-numbers.

Manning is the same for them both, although I think keeping a Red on the glove is generally easier because it is a bigger bird and not so prone to throwing itself about. The Harris can have its moments. Training, too, is the same formula for them both. But the Harris is clued in, and far more willing to move its carcass and show willing. Reds have that '*buteo*' mannerism - in their own time.

In East India and Pakistan they used to use an item called a 'guddi', which is a cloth cloak which completely covered both wings so the bird was effectively in a straight jacket. During this phase of between seven and ten days, the bird could observe and become habituated to its new surroundings. Often the hawk was tethered on a large straw mat in a public place, such as a market or a village square, under the watchful eye of the owner. Obviously the bird was very vulnerable and had to be watched at all times. Thankfully, as far as I am aware, the guddi didn't reach these shores.

Introducing The Dog

If you intend hunting with a dog (some do – some don't) my suggestion is to start the manning with your pet nearby at all times. Exposure is the key, so the bird sees the dog as a friend, not dinner. The bird must understand that it will be part of its life in a three-way team, and that is non-negotiable. If you are free-lofting the bird before you start the manning, make sure they can see each other. Then have the dog close when the bird is eating, to show it has no intention of stealing its food. I'm sure the bird will do a lot of posturing and screaming initially, but over time, she will learn to live with her new buddy.

During this stage, sit on a chair and keep your dog on your lap, or by your side when you are working with a creance. Dogs are such agreeable friends because they don't ask questions. It's the bird that will be doing the asking, and the question will be: "Is this creature after my food?". You (and the dog) have to convince her that is not the case.

Jumping To The Fist

We start with jumping to the fist. Show a titbit on the glove for the bird to see – and you whistle. She will quickly understand what you want her to do, although that doesn't necessarily mean she will do it. Everything is done with patience. If you get stressed – the bird gets stressed – and you may as well call it a day. This is where the hours of manning gets you through this stage. You can try encouraging her with kind words, but she won't understand a word of it. But it may satisfy your own conscience that you are cheering her on.

The falconry books of the late 19th century suggested the bird should be taken into a dark room in candlelight, and both the falconer and the bird should not return to natural light until the hawk has fed from the fist, or fallen asleep. I have always thought there must have been a big box of matches nearby because each bate was sure to blow out the candle. The darkened room is still used today, but mainly for training the highly excitable Goshawk. Cleared of furniture that could damage the bird's feathers, the teacher and the pupil settle down for their evening of social bonding. The candle is replaced by the invention called ... the electric light … thank you Thomas Edison. The system works, but is it really necessary to go to those extremes to train a Harris? Your decision.

Bating is something that happens (mostly) beyond our control. It is annoying and exasperating, but nonetheless, with tolerance and restraint, we all get used to it. If the bird throws itself away from you (usually the case), the first priority is to lift her clear of the ground. The bird may get back on the fist herself, or more often it will need to be gently lifted back before she exhausts herself. Look at it this way, each time it happens think to yourself - at least it was for a reason, she is exercising her wings.

The first major test of dedication for the beginner is to get the bird to take that first bite. She may tug and tear the meat, but then in a show of contempt, flick it about the room. If there is no progress after 30 minutes, try again later. But once she tastes the meat, more often than not, she will be interested in taking more. There is no tried and tested rule – some eat within seconds – some can take three days.

After that initial test, comes jumping to the glove. Six inches at first, then when she finally jumps, let her eat then place her back on the perch. Do it again, and soon she will understand the process. Three or four times in quick succession and the routine is being formed.

First Steps With The Hood

The hood is a major piece of apparatus in the falconer's tool box. If your bird can't see, it has nothing to respond to, making it calm and composed. This is a huge advantage taking the bird into a situation you know will disturb her.

It is very important that the hood fits, and the two concerns are enough eye clearance, and gape fit. The contouring for the eyes is where the stitching is on the hood and there must be enough clearance for the bird's eyes. As I mentioned earlier, there is a general size for each subspecies of bird, but there is still no guarantee it will fit until it is tried. The hood is sized by measuring across the top of the bird, looking downward. A female Harris is about 2.3", a female Red 2.5", but I use the 'about' in the loosest term. A bad fit will have the bird's eyes weeping, and damage the cere. If it is too tight on the beak there is the threat that the bird may not be able to cast. I don't think it is difficult spotting a bird that is having discomfort. Try leaving it on the bird for 15 minutes or so, remove it, and the feathers should be settled and where they should be. If they are crushed and dishevelled, there is a problem.

Hooding a bird is not easy. If she is not used to the drama she will turn her head left and right; up and down; and backwards and forwards, and they often bate. Slipping it over the beak is a confidence thing that only comes with experience. Then you draw the braces with your right hand and your teeth (if you still happen to have teeth). Gums are not nearly as good, so teeth are a significant piece of kit.

Hoods are a show piece of skill, and many of them are genuine works of art. They attract the curious and the dim, in equal numbers. "Why is your bird wearing a crash helmet?" is the usual question. I try to be polite, always, but a couple of times I have responded with: "The car was full so she's come on her motorbike."

In the early stages when you take off the hood the first thing the bird should see is food, making the interaction a positive one.

You need to condition your bird so that it understands that when the hood comes off it is either going to be fed or flown. Then later in training the repetition creates a mental connection so the bird knows that when the braces are struck, she is going to go hunting.

Use the hood to your advantage, not simply a 'keep the bird quiet' piece of falconry equipment.

Meeting The General Public

Take your time and learn as you progress. I don't see a need for the novice to rush anything. Whether it's days, weeks, months – as long as the bird is fit, healthy and happy – and you are fit, healthy and happy - it doesn't matter.

The next stage involves introducing your bird to the general public. Always keep her arm's length away from other people. Don't let the public touch her, even if they ask permission. I know it is allowed at some falconry centres and displays, but (as personal choice) I don't like anyone pawing my birds. Unlike pets such as cats and dogs that love to be stroked, touch isn't a positive thing to them. Should my hawk strike out a foot and grab, then maybe the general public could regret their decision, and it's not something I need to worry about. If they want to paw something they can go buy a dog.

Those first steps out into the human world together will be daunting, for you both. If a vehicle passes by, I turn my back towards the car to shield the bird from the stress. No matter how well the day is going, they are never jubilant when fast moving objects are approaching, be it a car, cyclist, jogger, etc. Shielding the bird certainly helps. If she is about to bate, I place my fingers on her chest, switching her attention away from the noise of the car engine to have her thinking: "Why is he touching me?"

I also ask friends to keep a respectful distance and walk on my right side if they happen to be walking with me – the bird being on the left. She needs her own space.

Spend as much time together as you can. Even on days when the weather is bad, there is still an amount of interaction you could do. Weighing her, checking her general well being, feeding her on the fist. No matter what else she does that day, those minutes you have with her will be the most important - for yourself and the bird.

What Is Your Bird thinking?

Researchers now have an in depth knowledge of what raptors can see and hear, and I believe the time is close when they can fathom their thoughts and how they communicate. I don't believe the only thoughts going through a raptor's brain is food, and how to catch it. Sadly, until someone develops that magical 'machine', we can only speculate their thoughts and reasons.

Looking at some of the characteristics of intellect and communication, can we decide how clever our birds are?

1) **Humour.** Scientists believe that human laughter evolved from the distinctive panting emitted by our great-ape relatives during rough and tumble play. Laughing signalled that play was good fun and nobody was about to tear anyone's throat out. Can birds laugh? Some can imitate sounds, including laughing, but that is nothing more than mimicking. I don't see traces of humour in my birds, but that is from a human perspective. Parrots seem to find humour in things, and maybe mimicking sounds gives them a kick? The Steller's Jay reproduces the call of the Redtail, but nobody seems to know why.

2) **Affection.** The jury is out on the amount of attachment a raptor has for its owner. At times we believe it's there, and I hope it is, and hope is a good thing. Do we read the wrong signs? My European Eagle Owl would tuck its head under my chin, but realistically speaking, it was probably wanting to go to sleep. Owls can't see right in front of their faces, so cuddles and nibbles are their way of figuring out what is in front of them. Perhaps we read them the wrong way.

3) **Curiosity.** I see traces of curiosity every time I pick up my birds, but curiosity is what keeps them alive. They need to know what is about, exactly where it is, and what its intentions are.

4) **Territory.** In the wild, just about every bird and animal has a territory to defend. Birds safeguard their mating, feeding, nesting and roosting areas because it is their means of survival. I don't imagine they have to be clever to achieve it, just be more aggressive than their enemies.

5) **Migration.** Redtails are partial migrants, meaning some migrate and some don't. Those from Alaska, Canada and the northern Great Plains head south for the winter. It involves long and perilous journeys heading to a designated place, with arrival and departure dates remarkably consistent over years. They are prompted by environment cues that we know very little about, but it is a dangerous trip because migrations are the highest cause of mortality in both juvenile and adult Redtails. How intelligent does a Redtail need to be to successfully complete that journey? Research shows birds have a substance called magnetite, which is located just above their beaks. This is a mineral that the birds use to help them determine Earth's magnetic field. Apparently, they can navigate using true north, and head south using the Sun's position in the sky throughout the day.

6) **Problem-solving.** Are raptors capable of problem-solving like Crows? Harris Hawks are probably the closest we would get to it, but all birds have their own specialist designs for specific needs. The BBC programme 'Inside The Animal Mind' showed a wild Raven solve a complicated eight-part puzzle to get food. It involved a short stick, a long stick, and a few stones, and eventually, it got the food. A Harris is as intelligent as it needs to be, yet once it comes into contact with man, that is when the problem-solving starts. It is unknown territory and unnatural for a bird to have that relationship, yet they learn to fly to the fist, work with dogs and respect that someone is trying to help them. At this point I think we need to define the word 'intelligence'.

7) **Communication.** How do raptors communicate? Their brain size (comparable to their body size) is similar to apes. Suggesting they are intelligent, but on a different plane to ourselves. They aren't wired to our complex thinking, and we aren't wired to theirs.

It is difficult trying to strip away sentimentality and wishful thinking to get an understanding of the avian mind. Only human beings have language in the academic sense, an open-ended system of signs and sounds, yet we look for something similar in our birds. Researchers say it isn't there, but they haven't yet developed the equipment that can tell us what is in their brains. The dolphin has cultivated its own system of communicating, the unique ability to see with sound. It's called echolocation and it can "see" objects in the water via a sonar system that tells it the shape, speed, distance, size and direction of travel of whatever is around. That is only a recent discovery, showing we haven't even scratched the surface when it comes to animal research.

Every single day that I fly my birds I know what sort of mood they are in before I get them to the scales. I constantly whisper to them, as though there is a secret that only we are privy to. No matter how much evidence there is suggesting they are oblivious to it all, I am convinced they at least listen. They don't understand a word, but they are inquisitive. I believe my two Harris Hawks, in their own mode of cheeps and chatter, answer back. They will keep a conversation going, and one of them (Khan) insists on always having the last word.

This is called 'anthropomorphism' - when we give animals human characteristics. It is an inaccurate understanding of the biological process in the animal world. We look for human awareness and intelligence, when it isn't there. But we believe it is … or at least hope we can develop it. Our presence is not a natural thing to them, so we change it, and we condition them to it. To the point they get into a pattern when they actually look for us on a morning, probably just for breakfast, but none the less they are happy (in their own way) to see us.

I have a female Harris (not imprinted) that gets very jealous if I show any affection to my wife, such as a kiss before I take the bird hunting on a morning. The bird will throw a small tantrum, making it plain that she disapproves. For a raptor, that supposedly has no emotion, I find that difficult to explain.

Getting To Flying Weight

Birds, like athletes, must have enough fat reserves and energy to successfully move extremely fast. Close attention must always be paid to weight. If a previous owner gives you a flying weight (as they usually do) only use it as a guide, rather than the answer to all things Holy. Maybe your scales may differ with his; or perhaps the bird has never been flown while in his care. You must establish the weight yourself.

The weight will change from day to day because of quantity and quality. Food quantity is obvious - give the bird a full crop and it won't be moving off its perch next day. Food quality - never feed fatty food like Pigeon or Duck if you are dropping your bird down in weight.

The process needs to be gradual rather than food deprivation. Washed meat is perfect for reducing a bird's mass without starving it, if you can get your bird to eat it. Strips of beef should be soaked in warm water, taking out a lot of the protein. If too much is taken out and the meat goes white, some birds won't eat it. Never feed washed meat in a hunting environment, because some birds don't think it worthwhile to make the flight to the glove for a piece of tasteless meat that has no nourishment. Food is the answer to getting your bird back, but it is only a reward if the bird actually likes what is being offered.

Reaching that weight is everything. If the bird is too high in weight it will either break up your partnership and head off over the hills and far away; go self-hunting; or sit up in a tree pretending it doesn't know you.

If a bird is too low … it dies!

When To Use The Whistle

If you use a whistle, use it at every meal time. Personally I whistle with my mouth, rather than using an actual whistle, and that has its own advantages. You cannot lose it, and it is always at hand (metaphorically) rather than fishing about in the bag looking for it.

Whistle when you feed her, and that will condition her to associate it with food. I know some who whistle when food is presented; as the bird pulls at it; and when she swallows it. That is your choice, if you feel it will help.

When you reach the stage where she is flying on the creance (a long line of string), you only want her to come to you when you say the word. When you whistle – she should come. You don't want to walk ten yards, turn around, and have eight talons in your face. You train to the whistle, and right from the start, if she flies - she gets rewarded.

Flying With The Creance

When flying with the creance, stand sideways to the bird (facing right), hold out your gloved hand, and always grasp the food so the bird can see it, not hidden away in the gloved fist. You are looking at a flight of 30-50yds, and with discipline and patience, you should get that very soon.

Raptors, like humans, tend to look for ways to get more for less effort. Which brings us to 'reward'. Always reward a flight! Never get her to fly when you have no food to give, or she will feel short-changed. Harris Hawks will let you know what they think about it, and any animal trained to food, whether its a lion, killer wale or a monkey, will do the same.

In total contradiction to what I have just written, I know a guy who free-flies his Harris and calls it down to the fist (without offering food) and uses the glove as a vantage point. The bird has been trained that way, and he claims it works. Each to their own.

If your bird is bang-on flying weight, she should fly to you without much persuasion. If she doesn't fly, I wouldn't feed her. If I put my fist up and if my bird doesn't crouch and respond, I give her a few minutes and call her several times. If she still doesn't fly, I hide the food and we end the session. I will take her elsewhere, into another field, and we go through it all again. If the same thing happens, she is NOT at flying weight, and that is my fault. Food is showing her the benefits of cooperation, and if she cannot be bothered, she isn't hungry. Raptors know the consequences of giving up on the offer of a meal - if they were in the wild and didn't make the effort, they would be feeling sorry for themselves with an empty belly.

When you are learning the ropes, and you want to return home with the bird on your glove each day, routine is not a bad thing. I don't recommend it religiously, but for the novice in the early stages, it has its benefits. Wild birds of prey are creatures of habit, which is why they learn what is successful, and then create a pattern. Some falconers wear the same hunting jacket every day. I don't see any harm in it. I don't believe the bird only recognises that one coat, or a certain colour falconry bag, or a cap, but if you think it helps … go with what you are comfortable with.

Talking of caps, I bought a new flat cap and one of my Harris Hawks absolutely hated it! The first three times I wore it the Harris would fly down, take it off my head and fly up a tree. The third time the cap got stuck in the branches and I never got it back. The full-time score: Me 0 Harris 3.

Once the bird is flying 40-50yds on the creance with gusto and confidence, she is ready for the next step. For the final days leading up to the first free flight, I think a pattern is a good thing. Weighing, getting to the same hunting ground where you fly on the creance, and do what you normally do. The bird knows what is expected of it. Once out hunting, they become more tolerant of new and different hunting environments, and forgiving with unexpected distractions.

Working With Dogs

I have to admit I am no game dog expert. I am more the hedge-kicking "hit the bush hard with a stick" type of falconer who has a dog that does its best to help. It knows how to flush, and it has its own way of doing it, but it isn't a gun dog. The only dogs I ever used in falconry are my Jack Russell terriers. Although I feel we get it right to the best of our best abilities – I know others who do the flushing game far better. I have seen others work with spaniels, labradors and all manner of dogs, and I whole-heartedly admire their professionalism. So I introduce you to my close friend, Brian Russell.

Brian Russell:
"If I was asked what is the best breed of dog for hunting, I wouldn't hesitate in saying the pointer. They hunt with passion and common sense. The last thing you want is a dog that gets in the way, so you don't want one that retrieves. That is most important, or you will end up with a battle between dog and bird, which is sure to end up nasty.

"There are three pointers that are used in falconry - German short-haired, Brittany and wire-haired – and I prefer the Brittany because it is reluctant to retrieve. The other two can be trained that way, but it doesn't come naturally.

"You cannot buy a trained hawking dog. It will not understand what is required of it, until you train it. You should consider buying a puppy bred from working parents.

"I usually run two dogs together. If one comes to the point, then the second backs it.

"The dog is significant in falconry, but the bird and its flight is always more important than the actions of the dog. Handling the bird is difficult enough without worrying where the dogs are. I have electric collars put on mine because it can be very easy to lose them on the point.

"My favourite part of falconry is watching an experienced Redtail staring at the dogs waiting for a point, and preparing itself accordingly. The dogs know the game, and they know how to win. They don't suffer fools gladly.

"Flying a Redtail without a dog is difficult for me because I feel we are missing so many opportunities at rabbits. I don't flush half as good as my dogs, and the bird knows it.

"Pointing is not something you can teach your dog to do – it is inbred. But they need to be trained just like any other dog for obedience, when to sit, when to walk (always on the right side of the falconer) when to stay quiet, and when to flush.

"The scent of quarry drifts down wind so your dog must be worked into the wind or across it. If the scent is good they stop, then slowly walk forward 'stalking' until prey is in range. You need the dog to stop when you tell it. Your tone of voice is very important to it. Like with a bird, it's not what you say but how you say it. They must be disciplined to the point they don't chase sheep, or you would be better leaving the it at home. "How good the dog performs depends on how much quarry is in the area, but also the weather conditions. The scent of game travels further in damp weather than dry, and obviously better in a slight breeze. Longer grass is also better than short, and it goes without saying, more chance of finding game hidden."

CHAPTER TEN – TRAINING AND HUNTING

Preparing For The Hunt

Once the hawk has vanquished its initial fears of the falconer and overcome the exasperation of the sights and sounds of the world outside, it moves on to what it does best. Now that she is accepting food rewards that are placed on the glove, and jumping and flying greater distances to you, next you introduce the lure. The lure has some resemblance to the quarry the bird will be hunting, and it is usually accepted that the Harris Hawk and Redtail will initially be pursuing rabbits. If you are hoping to fly at birds, you should try and get hold of a pair of Magpie wings, and make your own. Rabbit lures in various forms (good and bad) are readily available on Ebay – Magpie wings, not so much.

At first the bird may take some convincing to do what is asked of it, but persevere. It will all come right in the end. I don't suppose the bird ever believes that the 'dummy bunny' is a real rabbit, but it will go along with the idea knowing there is a reward. Once she grabs the lure, make a fight of it by pulling the string and giving the bird a tussle. It needs to learn that in hunting conditions the live rabbit won't lift a white flag and surrender. Whenever it flies to the fake rabbit, and it does so convincingly, give it a significant food reward.

Lure coursing drag machines are available in various shapes and sizes, at a healthy price. I have seen home-made designs that do the job just as well. The tried and tested method is to buy a JP PowerTorque motor (which are available around £30) and screw it inside a strong wooden box. Fix a large spool of 70-100 meter thin multi-functional Polypropylene string on the torque end, fed through a strong eyelet screw to keep it steady as it feeds. You can even use a ground peg for added stability to the line. A rabbit lure is tied to the end of the line, garnished with meat. The system is powered by a small motorbike 12V battery. Everything can be stored in the same wooden container, a similar shape to a tool box.

If the bells haven't already been introduced, they should be attached during creance work. The bird needs to get used to the sound and feel of them, and you can even attach the telemetry too. Nothing should be left to chance when the big day comes when she flies free. She won't need the added pressure of wondering what the hell is tied to her tail or leg. She must be accustomed to all the furniture on the body.

For manual creance controlled training, tie a real rabbit or squirrel (dead of course) to a piece of string. Get someone to hide it in a bush, then as you and the bird come into view, get your accomplice to pull the animal into view for the bird to make a 'kill'. Of course it's the same as the dummy bunny lure, but a little bit more practicable.

Entering Your Bird At Game

There are four prime ways of 'entering' a bird at game, listed below:-

1) Entering – vantage point:

If you are happy everything is going to plan and the bird is flying 30 or 40 yards to you convincingly on the creance, the she is ready to fly completely free.

There are various ways of hunting, but for the Harris and Redtail, they have an in-built preference for a vantage point. It's in their genes. They know what they do best, and inevitably its done from a tree or a pole.

Find a promising spot, with rabbits a plenty, and cast your bird into an over-hanging tree. If you work with a dog, let the beast do the graft while you keep an eye on what is happening above.

2) Entering – shotgun:

As well as the 'vantage point', alternatively there is the 'shotgun' technique of flying from the gloved fist. This probably is more advantageous to the falconer than the bird, because you are stopping the bird from self-hunting. That gives you more control of the hunt, and it is particularly beneficial if your bird is in its first season.

It does have its down side - the bird doesn't have any height advantage flying from the glove - and I can promise you, it won't be as productive. The rabbit gains the advantage because the bird is usually the first to spot it fleeing the scene, and the bird has to wait two seconds for its master to get his/her head into gear and release the jesses. Two seconds can be, and usually is, a life-saver for a sprinting bob-tail. Here is an idea that I use for a quick release. I always carry a wooden walking-stick for beating, so I put a thin nail in the bottom and cut the head off and file it sharp. I put a small hole in each of the flying jesses made from an eyelet punch. When the bird is ready to be entered I put the nail through the jesses, and hold her securely. You are not holding onto the jesses with your gloved fingers, and it is easier to secure her firmly. The first sight of quarry, pull away the walking-stick and cast. I find this very beneficial on freezing cold winter days when my hands are almost blue I can hardly feel my fingers.

3) Entering – following on:

Another style of attack is for the bird to 'follow on'. My two Harris Hawks do this remarkably well. One knows the game so well, she flies in front and waits for the flush, while the other lags a few yards behind. Always loyal, they always stay tight.

There are many ways to teach this, like calling the bird along a line of fence posts, or from tree to tree. Keep her interested at all times. There are signs to watch out for, and if her mind starts to wander, that's the time to get her down. If she does that early in the hunt, she is not at flying weight. It's not the bird's fault, it is bad preparation.

4) Entering – out of the hood:

A lot of Eagle and Goshawk enthusiasts use this method but it works well with any bird that is used to the hood. The bird is sat on the glove and it's hood is removed at the sight of game. To train to this method, the bird understands that as soon as the hood comes off it will be required to bolt off the fist. This is coached in lure training, ideally with someone else pulling the lure as you remove the hood.

The priority is not the game in the bag, it is getting home with your prize possession, ready to fight another day. Always remember those very words when you are in two minds and considering taking chances with your bird. In life we tend to regret the chances we didn't take, but in falconry sometimes there is no second chance to put things right.

Your bird will now have the instinct to hunt and should know the basics of what to do. You have to convince her that working as a team is beneficial. Nothing is more fun to a raptor than catching prey, but the aim is to teach her that she needs you (and maybe a dog) to help her do it.

Now is the time … let's go hunting.

Maiden Kill

Entering is the most challenging time for a beginner. First you decide what is expected of the bird and what you want it to do. Catch game is the obvious answer, but before that she must be fit, happy, in good feather and responsive to cues.

I know the thoughts that go through the head of an apprentice, because I feel it every time I introduce a new bird. That first flight, that dramatic moment is always like the first time. Letting go of the jesses is exhilarating, but it is like that feeling before a parachute jump. It is always more stimulating when it is over and you shout "I've done it!" And you have done it right.

Remember, if the groundwork has been done, you should have nothing to fear. Spectacular achievement is always preceded by unspectacular preparation. You have worked hard, now experience the reward.

A hawk must have a strong desire to chase quarry, and that is not always a 'given'. The same goes for catching and holding onto the prey. That, too, is not necessarily part of every raptor's make-up. I've heard a lot of excuses for missed opportunities: "It's a nice Redtail but it has 'near miss syndrome'. You cannot rid a hawk of that."

'Near miss syndrome' is not a virus you need a face mask for, it is not Covid-19. Nor is it picked up by getting too close to fellow falconers. I don't even think such a syndrome even exists. It's a term for a bird that hits a rabbit on the backside, rather than the head, and is kicked off before it makes the kill. Or landing on the ground holding a foot full of feathers, as the Pheasant vanishes into cover.

I know young birds can get discouraged very quickly, which could be poor training or even poor genes. What they need is plenty of exposure to suitable quarry in their early flights. That maiden kill is priceless. There is nothing like immediate (and frequent) success in the field to breed faith and belief.

There can be a big variation in the persistence of individual birds when going in for the kill. Some experienced Harris Hawks can be opportunistic, refusing a difficult slip in the belief there will be another one along in a minute. Is it laziness knowing the chances of taking 'that' particular quarry was extremely doubtful, or intelligence? Opportunism is a learned demeanour. An old, experienced hawk may not fly out of the blocks with the same reckless abandon as a bird in its first season.

When entering for the first time I don't change the food leading up to that first hunt. Many falconers believe the meal the day before should be rabbit meat with nothing that could form a casting. No fur or bones. This allows everything to pass straight through the bird so she is empty of indigestible materials before the big day.

There are the obvious procedures:- look at the weather forecast for the coming day; the telemetry should be tested and new batteries fitted; and all spare equipment positioned in the bag. There is no guarantee the weather forecast will be right. Is it ever? But it gives some indication, and an excuse to incriminate the weather forecasters for getting it wrong. We don't need torrential rain or strong winds to contend with. We want land that is rich with quarry, and the right weather to encourage the rabbits to be out and about. Get out first light when there is more chance the rabbits are active.

The decision to go ahead rests with you. If the weather is bad; the bird is acting up; or your gut feeling says something isn't right – leave it for another day. It's not excuses, it is common sense, and it is your call.

Helen Macdonald writes in her award winning book 'H is for Hawk': "I once flew a Harris Hawk free after four days," but my advice is – don't even go there! The lady has earned her stripes training Goshawks and I'm sure she is a wizard with the glove, quite possibly the Harry Potter of the falconry world. But don't be afraid of growing slowly. Don't watch the clock – do what it does – keep going.

It is so important to be away from roads, vehicles and people. Trees should be empty of leaves, preferably without evergreens, so your bird cannot go into hiding. Replace mews jesses with field jesses and try a trial flight to the glove to ensure her mindset is right. You need that established relationship in tact, and you need the confidence to trust it. Set her up in a tree, and when she is settled (hopefully bobbing her head), prepare your dog. Get to work beating brush and hopefully something flushes. Always keep an eye on your bird and check that she is showing an interest. Give her every advantage. A hawk cannot be expected to fly up-wind at anywhere near the speed of a running rabbit, and don't cast directly downwind for obvious reasons. Birds are aero-dynamic, rabbits aren't. However, rabbits don't get as much force against them at ground level, but birds need to work with the thermals to gain speed for a kill. She is sure to pass up one or two rabbits, so don't be disappointed when it happens.

If you are working with a dog, it is important you make sure it is under control. It can be dangerous if it runs in on a catch, so if the bird gets its prey, make-in with the dog on its leash.

I have constantly talked about rabbits as the main quarry but Pheasants can be great game. I had a female Harris that took twice as many Pheasants as rabbits in one season, and just about cleaned out the local shoot. It got to the point when those poor gun-slingers had nothing to fire guns at! I would hunt the farm Monday to Friday, and the guns would 'pop' on a weekend. Sadly, after about four weeks or so, I was told by the farmer my darling bird wasn't welcome any more. I lost the land, but I felt it was inevitable. It was like giving a child free-reign in a sweet shop.

Redtails are a bit more difficult to introduce to Pheasant than the Harris, but never underestimate their power and endurance. It's difficult to give them a good 'slip' from the fist because they lose those two seconds (that I mentioned earlier) getting that kick off the glove. Without question they perform better from a vantage point. If the Pheasant takes cover, a Red will go on a quest, through the thickest bramble and undergrowth in pursuit. They may lack the sharpness off the glove but they excel in persistence.

'Shooting Season' Dates

Pheasant Oct 1 – Feb 1
Partridge Sept 1 – Feb 1
Red Grouse/Ptarmigan Aug 12 – Dec 10
Black Grouse Aug 20 – Dec 10
Duck/Goose (inland) Sept 1 – Jan 31
Duck/Goose (below high water) Sept 1 – Feb 20

The Trade Off

Once your bird latches onto its quarry, you make in and do a trade-off. The creature may need despatching, and with your bird trying to squeeze the life out of it, this can be difficult for the apprentice. It's not so much knowing what to do, it's getting everything together. You don't want the bird to feel you are robbing her of her catch, but you need to make sure the prey doesn't escape. In theory you would approach with a trade-off piece of meat on the glove or the lure, and make it more appealing than the creature she has hold of. That is a tough ask.

Raptors instinctively start eating, whether the catch is dead or alive. So you need to anchor the rabbit by a hind leg before it gets any chance of freedom. Then you need to dispatch the prey with a sharp knife, cervical dislocation or thoracic compression. Your bird should jump for the trade-off and you discreetly hide the prey in the bag.

The golden rule is never try and tare the catch away from your bird. I learnt that lesson in my early years when I tried to wrestle a rabbit away from my Ferruginous. The bird didn't have a secure hold and was losing its grip. I hung onto it as it slipped from the bird's grasp, and I got a foot in the face from my dear bird for the help I was giving it. I still have that scar to this day.

Remember, the bird is in killing mode, highly sensitive, and nothing like the little darling that sits so content on its bow perch in the garden. There is a difference in attitude and approach.

Doing the trade-off is how it is normally done, but if it's the first kill, I believe the bird deserves to feed on it. Open it up and let her enjoy her magical moment, while you enjoy yours. Afterwards, secure her, swap the 'furniture' back to mews jesses and leash her to the glove.

This is where a large bag comes in handy. Hiding chicks or meat from the eyes of the bird, and for sneaking inside whatever you have just caught, while the hawk is otherwise occupied. There are detachable game bags that work extremely well and are readily available on the internet. But when it comes to falconry bags, I have bought some rubbish over the years. What looked good on a photograph never arrived at the door. You live and learn, and the bag I use now is that customised laptop shoulder bag that I mentioned in an earlier chapter. Check them out. Be warned, it probably won't be appreciated amongst the aristocracy of the sport because it's not regimental. But I stopped doing things regimental a long, long time ago.

Self-Hunting

All hawks are usually adaptable to the alternating terrain, and adopt different flight styles in contrasting weather. So, having them hunt from different vantage points is logical. Flying from the glove, from high trees, T-perch or soaring, they all have a place in the falconer's locker.

This is where falconry styles may differ. Some like having their hawk sit tight, under control at all times. Usually in a confined area when the hawk may have to be recalled quickly because of dog walkers or whatever. Obviously using this method means there is less chance of losing your bird. However, others prefer to give their bird complete freedom, called 'self-hunting'. This means the bird selects where it wants to go and how it wants to hunt. The alternative to following-on, the falconer follows the bird.

A hawk has more situational awareness than the falconer. It will spot quarry quicker, and if given freedom, it will learn how to position itself to the maximum advantage. This means you rely heavily on the telemetry system. If they know the lie of the land they can head off out of sight, knowing there is better and easier game over a hill. All well and good if that hill is where you are allowed to go. Not so good if it isn't.

Flying A Cast

One of the main reasons why the Harris Hawk is so popular worldwide is the fact that it can be flown in a 'cast'. That means two (or more) can be flown together at the same time. Numbers are normally drawn at a field meeting to decide the order that birds are flown, but the Harris has made the sport so 'neighbourly' that Harris guys meet together and set their birds away at the same time.

Is it a difficult task trying to control two birds and a dog? Personally I don't attempt it single-handed. I always prefer it one-person-one-bird, so hunting is no more demanding than any other hunt.

If you intend flying birds together it is important that their social skills are more than just good, they need to be impeccable. A hawk needs proper manners around people, dogs, and particularly, other Harris Hawks. Your bird must never be hostile and show aggression and territorial behaviour towards other hawks.

In training I believe the birds benefit from being within view of each other at all times. They can lose that relationship if they are not housed and flown regularly. I like to perch my two hunting birds close on the weathering ground, but not to such an extent they can reach one another. They must stay familiar. I also put them together through the moult. Long term isolation maybe acceptable with other birds, but not with a pair you work together in a cast.

Bonding a male and female together gives you the best in all situations in the field. I am always asked the difference between flying males and females, but putting them together demonstrates the two contrasting styles. Males are quicker in acceleration and turning, because of their nippy size, but only over a short distance. A female is quicker over a long haul, and far stronger flying into a strong wind. Males have less attitude towards dogs and humans, because they are down in the pecking order when they fly in groups in the wild. They seem to know their place instinctively. Females can be more relaxed and amiable than males during the manning process and training, but the female is the boss in a cast.

At first I thought my pair would compete to get to quarry first, but they don't. They both know when a rabbit is there, and they constantly communicate with each other. They time their swoop accordingly. They don't fight over who gets the rabbit first, they simply back each other up and cooperate in whatever it takes to perform the kill. It works incredibly well, particularly in heavy cover.

Hunting With Ferrets

It's a personal opinion, but I think of all raptors, the Redtail is the best bird to work with ferrets. A fellow hawker of mine even goes as far as to call them an "essential partnership".

If the bird is in its first year, I would suggest the ferret should look as much 'unlike' a rabbit as possible. Which is why I prefer albinos because they are so distinctive when they emerge from a hole. You, and your bird, could never mistake an albino for a rabbit.

Ferrets need considerate handling and attention. Selection is important because not all enjoy working with a bird. They are capable of making the hawk look good with plenty of slips, but a bad ferret will ruin your day. They do what they do, and don't need training, it's the bird that needs the instruction (and education) not to attack it.

Ferrets come in many different colour varieties, and the males (called hobs) are far bigger than the females (called jills). They are domesticated, have an excellent sense of smell, and usually can tell when a warren is inhabited. They are intelligent and loving animals, but they are a predator at heart and can be very aggressive if mishandled. They have a nasty bite and can lock their jaws just as ferocious as a hawk can lock its feet. They will hang on for as long as they feel the need.

Ferrets are instinctively inquisitive and don't need much schooling to go looking for rabbits. But the secret of success is to keep the hunger level at the right point. If they are not hungry, they won't be interested and may fall asleep down the warren. Too hungry and they tend to kill the rabbit down the hole, and keep it there. Always take a spade with you. You will need to buy a tracking system that will help locate the position and the depth that you will be digging when they go AWOL.

Lamping

Lamping can be a controversial subject amongst the purist in the game, some suggesting night hunting should be left to owls. It is a way of getting game, without question, but the flights are rarely as spectacular as ones during the day.

You need a powerful lamp, and one of the best lamps to use is the Tracer T612v rechargeable hand-held LED spot light. Check it out.

The Harris Hawk tends to take to lamping a lot quicker than the Redtail, but that's not to say the Red can't do it. Not all birds delight in working to the lamp, and I can include owls in that. My Bengal Eagle Owl was particularly disappointing, forever wanting to get off the fist as though she had an advantage over me and wanted to prove it. She would make for rabbits at twilight, no question, but she didn't like the lamp. Let's be honest, she didn't need it, the lamp was for us idiots stumbling around in the dark.

In training, throw food (and the lure) into the beam, then recall the bird to the fist. In daytime the Red will usually catch rabbits with more fight than the Harris, but the 'no holds barred' direct style isn't as adaptable for night flying. The Harris tends to float up, following the rabbit from above, waiting for its chance. While the Red sticks to the beam, the Harris often disappears from view until she hits the prey.

The secret is to keep the beam on the rabbit at all times. If the bird flies down through the beam of light things can go wrong just before the moment of impact. The closer it gets to the target, its own body shape casts a shadow and the bird can lose sight of the prey in the darkness. As the guy holding the bird, I always prefer to be 20yds or so away from the guy holding the beam. He/she shines a light, I cast the bird from the side, and there is no shadow on the kill.

Lamping is convenient for those who work during the day and don't see much light (if any) during the winter months. If you work long days and object to being called a 'weekend falconer', this could be for you.

Although landowners may not begrudge you 'accidentally' taking the odd pheasant, they don't want you cleaning out their entire stock. So they may even prefer you wandering the fields at night knowing you are after vermin rather than their precious game.

CHAPTER ELEVEN – LOST BIRDS

Let me introduce you to 'Goldie', the Golden Eagle that escaped from London Zoo in 1965. It was an event, played out live on TV, that made a huge impression on my father. After 12 days of news reports, and falconers from far and wide joining in the hunt, the Eagle was finally captured uninjured. My father, who was enthusiastically willing the bird to stay 'un-captured', thought it was a degrading spectacle for such a noble and magnificent creature. Following the incident, he was convinced birds of prey were never meant to be domesticated and should never be kept behind bars.

He said at the time: "Birds like that either die or escape, because they aren't meant to be caged."

A few years later, when I took up falconry, I expected some opposition from him. It didn't come ... well, not at first. I took care of a couple of injured Kestrels and returned them to the wild, which he found commendable. Then the big guns started arriving. The Goshawks, Eagle Owls, Ferrugenous etc and we were in a different ball park to the humble little Kestrel. He was horrified at the amount of money I spent on a Finnish Goshawk, but looking back, he was right and I needed my head examined for paying so much.

He made his feelings felt: "That money goes up in the air every time you fly it. What if it flies off?"

That quote, more than any other, made me determined to succeed in falconry. I was never going to lose a bird … ever! Just to prove to my dad I was in control.

By good luck or good management, it took a lot of years before I was unfortunate enough to experience that feeling of loss. Sadly my father passed away many years before I lost a bird, so he never got the chance to hear me say: "On that occasion you were right dad."

Why things go wrong

There are many reasons for 'misplacing' a bird, and not all of them the falconer's fault. Defective equipment is probably top of the list. But sometimes you have to hold up your hand and admit it was plain and simple carelessness. Nothing is more dangerous to a bird than flying off with a leash still attached, because the person in charge had a moment of brain-freeze. That is the worst case scenario, and unless the bird is found within hours the prospects of getting it back are bleak.

Let's first look at the equipment failures. Telemetry defect is not common, but it can happen. It can be a dangerous piece of apparatus because falconers do tend to rely on it a little too much at times. When I was first introduced to the sport nobody had a tracker on their bird, because they hadn't been invented. The flying weight was more critical then, because we didn't have a safety net. How ironic that I never lost a bird in those days, but I did with a tracker! Batteries can fail; the battery connection can fail; or the telemetry transmitter can get dislodged. Whatever … you have a lost bird.

What else can go wrong? I mentioned the swivel earlier. It is a small piece of metal, but if the button head becomes broken, the bird is off on its own. However, that is so rare it is hardly worth mentioning.

I don't regard split jesses as apparatus failure, more ignorance, because they should be checked every single day. The same goes for leash buttons.

Everything else that goes wrong is usually in the excitement of a hunt and chasing game. One other unusual circumstance is the bird that can undo a falconer's knot. Something very rare, I admit, but I have seen footage of a Harris Hawk (on CCTV) that could do it. Just to prove it was no fluke, it did it once again. Most raptors chew on jesses, bewits, leashes and anything that happens to be attached to their feet – but keep an eye on any bird that focuses on the knot. As the saying goes: "If a monkey taps at a typewriter for long enough it will write the complete works of Shakespeare." If a Harris Hawk picks at a falconer's knot often enough, it will find the solution to the riddle.

There is no shame if a bird heads off in the course of a flight, on the assumption every precaution was in place before it happened. But many of us have flown birds slightly over flying weight, to keep the bird exercised, in the belief that telemetry will be the saviour should something go wrong. Occasionally we can be pressured into putting on a demonstration for the benefit of friends when weather conditions are far from ideal, and I am the one holding up my hand here. It's dumb, and all the more painful when those very friends are on hand to witness your stupidity.

Then there is the pure lunacy of letting go of the leash; not tying a knot well enough; opening the mews door and the bird flies past; changing jesses from mews to flying jesses and the bird is spooked; all the things that shouldn't go wrong … but have been known to.

Birds get lost, so you go find them!

Getting Your Bird Back

Should the bird veer off on a hunt, the first thing to do is to watch where she is heading. Get some sort of baring and keep it in sight for as long as you possibly can. Some birds will head back in the direction they have just flown from to look for the owner, and then your problem is solved. Birds that fly off to unknown territory usually sit tight feeling sorry for themselves, having missed an opportunity at game. However, should your bird get its quarry, it will drag it somewhere to hide from other opportunist birds and animals. It is then that it is important to find where she is, because a bird with a full crop is in no urgency to return to anywhere.

I had a Harris make in on a hare but she was kicked off (and somehow lost her tracker), then in pure frustration chased after a Wood Pigeon. They flew through the dense wood, then up and over a large building, and I lost sight. I found out later (from a dog walker) that she caught the pigeon half a mile further on and took it into someone's garden to eat. The hunt was on. Harris Hawks never fly far, yet she had me on a merry goose-chase for weeks. What kept me going was the story of a guy who lost his Goshawk and then it returned eight years later. I always had the belief I would get my bird back.

The days past by and a few dog-walkers caught sight of her, or heard the bells, but always in thick woods. There were many false alarms, kind people trying to help but mistaking a crow for a hawk. If you can see your bird, you are halfway to recovering it. The land (about five miles square) was littered with rabbits, she was well trained, and I never doubted she could take good care of herself. Every time anyone saw her she was on the move. She would make an appearance, then disappear into the undergrowth. Then on day 87, I was flying a Ferrugenous in the same woods, and I cast her into a tree. Suddenly, that very same Harris flew straight at me and landed on a fence no more than 10yds away. I placed a chick in my gloved hand and held it out, more as a gesture than any belief she would fly to me. Then almost three months since I last held her, she flew to the fist, as though those 87 days hadn't happened. She was below flying weight with war scars on her feet and head, yet she returned as manned as the day she left. I wrapped her up in my coat and tied the Ferrug to the glove, then returned home looking as though I was carrying a bundled up ET. Happiness comes in waves - buying her, training, flying and devoting my time. But no feeling was as beautiful as the day she came back.

That is a message … never give up on a lost bird. If the plan doesn't work – change the plan – but keep looking!

Tips On What You Will Need

As you search, any help from extra bodies will increase your odds of getting your bird back. The more people the better, everyone keeping in touch by mobile phones. Listen for the bells or notice how other birds are acting in the area, particularly Blackbirds who scald anything threatening with their warning call. Crows and Seagulls virtually pin-point any danger by mobbing.

Harris and Redtails tend to prefer dead trees to sit in as a vantage point, but not when they are full of food. Then they hide. Sat on a vantage point, your bird will see you long before you see it, but when they hide, they do a very good job of it.

When you finally do spot her, try calling her down with food and a lure, but give her an easy path to reach you. Never stand directly under the tree, because she won't drop like a stone. You need to give it flying space. If it sits tight, as it is sure to with a full crop, you have a problem. If dusk is setting in, the bird won't go far, for sure. You could try climbing the tree and grabbing it, or use a landing net, but to be honest, I've never seen that work. The bird gets spooked and flies to another tree. You either spend the night under that tree, or head home and return before the sun rises.

A well manned bird will remain tame, even towards strangers, for some time. You can look on the local Facebook websites, or even place a post asking if anyone has seen (or heard the bells) of a bird of prey. This works incredibly well, and I often get calls or messages from people asking: "Have you lost your bird? I've seen a big hawk in my garden." It is usually a wild Sparrowhawk or Buzzard, but it's nice when people show concern.

A lost Harris Hawk usually doesn't fly far, and they are generally found quickly. Redtails cover a larger area because they are naturally soaring birds, but only if they have been flown that way and the area is open land. If they have only been entered in confined woods, they will stick there. If, and when, they move on depends solely on the availability of food.

Binoculars are an essential part of the kit when looking. I carry business cards in my bag with my address and phone number. I give them to anyone I think can help - dog walkers, farmers, joggers, whoever treads the walkways and fields where the bird could be. I ask them to phone me immediately if they see anything that resembles a lost hawk. You are sure to get false alarms, because kind people genuinely want to help you the best they can, and show willing. Then any hawk they see seems lost. However, all it takes is one sighting that can result in you getting your bird back.

When a bird is lost, a tail bell is always better than legs bells. A bird can go a long time sat in a tree without moving a muscle … apart from flicking its tail. Telemetry has advanced considerably in the last couple of decades, but as a friend of mine often says: "Will telemetry ever be a substitute for bells?" He says that tongue-in-cheek, but bells are very important.

Phoning the RSPCA could be a good idea. I have seen them go beyond the call of duty rescuing trapped and injured birds, and I cannot praise them enough. The RSPB (Royal Society for the Protection of Birds), however, usually don't want to know. They are the same with injured birds, because they don't have facilities to take care of them. They are usually too busy setting up hides in the Cairngorms watching Ospreys, or in the Norfolk Broads looking for Great Crested Grebes. That is where the money goes. When injured birds of prey are handed into the police or RSPB they usually end up with a falconer, and I was getting on average of five a year. Everything from Little Owls to Short Eared Owls; Sparrowhawks to Common Buzzards, their food (and keep) financed by myself. Meanwhile the RSPB get financial grants from far and wide. I'm not alone in taking in wild birds and releasing them when they are well, because the majority of falconers do the same.

If you can see your bird, but it refuses to come down to you from a tree, there is a technique called 'winding up' that is worth a try. I have seen people attempt it, yet I have never seen anyone have any success with it. There is always a first time!

In a nutshell, 'winding up' is getting your bird to fly down to a lure, and as the bird is eating, you walk around and around in a circle holding the line until the feet of the bird is tangled. The shorter the grass the better chance of a positive result, otherwise the line gets snarled in undergrowth rather than the hawk's legs.

I think using a trap can be more successful, but we walk a fine line in the UK because most of them are illegal. Falconers in the US are far more experienced than us at using traps because there traps ARE legal. It is accepted that USA falconers will trap a passage bird (usually a Redtail) in the autumn, hunt with her throughout the winter and spring, and release it for the breeding season. Trapping is what they do best.

There are various forms of bird traps used in the States, but the commonest one is the 'noose-trap', which is live quarry (pigeon, rodent or small rabbit) in a wire cage covered in wire or nylon nooses. It is illegal to use 'bagged' game in the UK, so a dead creature would have to be the bate. The principal is simple enough, the bird flies down to get its free meat, tries to batter its way through the wire mesh, and ends up caught by the foot. It works, but it is very much trial-and-error because someone has to be quick off the mark to get to the bird before it breaks free. The cage must be pinned to the ground securely with metal spikes or tent pegs, because the bird will try and carry it away, and a Redtail would have no problem doing that. If the bird does get it airborne (and is caught in a noose) the problem escalates.

Another trap is the bow net, which is made from strong, light, plastic mesh. It is usually circular but I prefer the rectangular shape. The idea is to place the quarry in the middle, then when the bird flies down to take it, pull a line (connected to metal rods fixed to two large staples) and the mesh flips over the top. It works well, but takes quite a while to set up. If you know the region where the bird has been spotted, try setting up before first light.

There is also a portable contraption called the Larsen trap, which again is bated with quarry. The hawk will drop down through the hole on the top and the mechanism closes behind it.

CHAPTER 12 - HEALTH AND DISEASE

Coping

In the wild, birds naturally trim their own beak by eating bones, stripping meat off dead carcasses, and shaping it on branches or rocks. That doesn't always happen in captivity. I always provide wood branches, but that is never enough. So we have to 'cope' the beak ourselves.

Just like human finger and toe nails, the bird's talons and beak are constantly growing. If they can trim them naturally, obviously is is best to encourage them. For example, when I take my Redtail out close to my home, there is a massive decorative rock close to a field where I exercise her. She loves to sit on it, she feels as though she is something special, and trims her beak. It's like a make-do, rough and ready beauty parlour.

Talons usually take care of themselves if the bird is hunting regularly. They are the weapons that bag the game, and I am of the mindset 'the bigger the better.' But occasionally they need the odd trim.

According to 16th century terminology: "Falcons have talons; hawks have claws." I have never known an austringer talk about the "claws" on his/her

Goshawk. These days raptors have talons and cats have claws. I once asked a friend the question, "If falcons have talons, and hawks have claws, what do eagles have?" The guy stood holding his elegant Golden Eagle, the bird perched high on his excessively large glove. He glanced down at the eight flick-knives on the end of eight super strong yellow toes, and paused to take a moment to think before replying: "What about flippers?" The wise live with their wisdom, as the fool becomes king.

Trimming the hook of the beak is done with nail or dog clippers and finished off with small craft files.

More terminology for you - on the upper mandible of a falcon at each side is a small, sharp piece of beak called the 'tooth'. The curved parts in the same place on hawks and Buzzards are called the 'festoon'.

Trimming the tip of a beak and filing it is easy enough, as long as it isn't cut to extreme and end up bleeding. No more than a quarter of an inch. Trimming the underside of the mandible (if it overgrows) is a lot more difficult. I would use a thin file rather than sharp knives or clippers.

I have heard of some falconers using miniature electric files. Dremel is popular in the States, but it must be used with caution, and only by experts. I'm sure those devices produce excellent results in the right hands, but it must be very easy to make a mistake. Get it wrong and it is sure to cause injury and deformity.

Imping

It is common for primary feathers to get damaged for all manner of reasons, but chiefly when the bird is flying free in a mews with metal fencing, or the mews is smaller than the wing span of the bird. Whenever this happens the broken part should be cut off, and the feather 'imped'.

You will need spares, which are usually acquired during the moult, or maybe a donation from a fellow falconer. I have seen people willing to buy them with adverts on falconry forums.

Carbon fibre imping kits are available from Crown Falconry (as well as many other on-line suppliers) with a guide that helps you through the process.

Once a feather has fully grown it is dead. They are hollow towards the end that goes into the bird's flesh. The two hollow ends of the old feather and the new one can be joined by means of a pin or a plug. The carbon fibre imping pins come in three sizes, with size 2 (1 mm, 1.5 mm, 2 mm) suitable for the Harris and Redtail. They can be bonded with most epoxy adhesives. If you need to shorten the pins, do not use pliers or nippers as they will split the end of the pin. Cut with a junior hacksaw or a sharp craft knife.

It takes two people – one to hold the bird, the other to perform the procedure. Hood the hawk, have a table ready and a soft cushion. Personally, I do it outside on the lawn so the bird cannot bate and hurt itself. Get the assistant to hold the bird firmly, in the traditional manner, with his/her hands over the hawk's body with palms downwards and the thumbs joined. The tips of the fingers should be towards the hawk's tail, and the wrists over the hood. Get a firm grip around the upper part of the wings and the thickest part of the body, holding the bird firmly on the cushion.

Obviously the new feather needs to be the same length and shape as the one it is replacing, having occupied the same station in the wing, or the same place in the tail. The feather is dead so the bird feels no pain. With the forefinger and thumb of the left-hand (if you are right-handed), take hold of the damaged feather just above the place of damage, and separate it carefully from the other feathers. Then (with the right hand) use a Stanley knife or craft knife and cut obliquely upwards along the web of the feather on its thinner side until the edge cuts the shaft just above the breakage. Measure it with the new feather and cut it exactly. Feathers are hollow, and the idea is to pin and glue the new feather to the old.

Instructions will be included in the kit. It can be a more awkward procedure, than difficult. Using a quick-drying adhesive means you have only one crack at getting it right. It is not really 'trial and error', so I would always recommend that a novice watches someone perform the task before trying it him/herself.

The difficult part is getting the two halves to fit together in relation to those adjacent, without spilling surplus glue onto other feathers. Superglue is impressive stuff, but it dries incredibly quickly.

Moulting

All birds moult annually, in a gradual process that sees them replace old feathers with new. It lasts around five or six months when the bird 'drops' a couple of primaries at a time, and down feathers along the way. The slow development of growth allows the bird to be able to fly at all times.

The moult starts around April, when hunting is at an end and the breeding season starts for both the quarry, and the bird.

Moulting time is generally accepted by most falconers as the time to give their birds a rest. But in the wild, hunting goes on as normal. Birds nest and raise chicks and their parents work tirelessly to feed them, while replacing feathers at the same time. It is a natural process, common to most creatures on the planet. It's not some sort of deadly 'Amazon swamp rat disease' that some falconers seem to fear. Birds can be flown at this time, and it will not harm the bird's health. I don't believe in locking a bird away for six months without human contact. Some are locked away to breed, but that is different entirely. A single bird needs contact with the outside world, and not be stuck in a prison. The dispute over the rights and wrongs will go on as long as man flies birds. My birds are kept in their weather ground; picked up daily; treated like one of the family; and (apart from not hunting) life goes on as normal. The conventional day-to-day routine doesn't affect how the feathers grow.

A Harris and Redtail have ten primary feathers in each wing, and 12 tail feathers. Those are the 32 that could potentially be 'imped' should they break or bend.

If you want to go all biological and zoological, the five types of feathers are:

1) Down
2) Semiplume
3) Filoplume
4) Contour
5) Bristle.

The question I get asked often is: "What happens if you continue to fly the bird through the moult?" Keeping a bird at flying weight will not kill it, but the course of moulting slows down. Rather than five months to replace the entire set, it could take eight, or in some cases the bird doesn't moult at all. That is extreme. Usually when the bird is given rest the pattern commences again. Many falconry centres that gives flying demonstrations tend to have their birds moult in the winter, because the summer is their busiest time for custom.

A time-out period for the bird, with a good diet, vitamins and rest, produces stronger feathers. A bird of prey has specific nutritional needs. Although keeping its diet as close to what it would eat in the wild is acceptable, research has shown that in captivity there are additives we can provide that can (and will) prolong its life.

'Raptor Breeder Essentials' is a calcium based food vitamin powder usually given to young chicks to help with their growth during the breeding season. But it is a calcium boost for birds that are a bit under the weather or going through the moult. One pinch on a day old chick is all that is needed.

Poor feathers can have 'fret marks' or 'hunger trace,' which is a line that looks as though it has been cut with a sharp knife. It is a weak point that is easy to spot, and raptors are not alone, other birds get it too. Although 'hunger trace' speaks for itself (the bird not getting enough high protein food when the feathers are growing), some argue it is not a hunger problem at all. They suggest the 'hunger trace' is stress related. We have to understand that birds of prey are highly sensitive, finely tuned, complex creatures that do suffer from stress. I have noticed such marks when a bird has changed home and owner, and we all know how stressful we feel when we move house. A hawk in confinement relies exclusively on its owner, and when that person disappears from its life, anxiety can lead to trauma. A hawk doesn't ask for much, but take it away, and there can be a mark left behind, quite literally.

Local Vet

A good vet is significant to the well-being of your new bird. Things changed in veterinary circles when falconry grew to its present status in popularity. Of course licensed vets have incredible knowledge of cats and dogs, but 50 years ago, produce an unwell raptor and most didn't know its cere from its crop. One young vet proudly told me that she had worked with wild Kestrels quite often, and my European Eagle Owl (which was almost big enough to look her in the eye) would be in safe hands. She believed her experience would shine through, when inwardly I feared the worst. After piecing screams from the examination room, an ambulance was called, and I had to find another vet.

I would suggest you talk to falconers in the area and find out which veterinary surgeon is the most raptor-friendly and make a note of the number. It is always best to have it at hand quickly, should an emergency arise.

Keeping Your Bird healthy

An experienced falconer can spot when a bird is unwell within seconds. It's not that difficult. The tell-tale signs are identical to everything I explained in chapter six about what to look for when buying a new bird.

A flourishing hawk will have bright round eyes, sit with a foot tucked under its feathers, preen often, and be alert and attentive to what is going on around it. If something is wrong you must be quick to notice it.

The other two key signs of illness are discoloured mutes and ill-formed castings. If either of these symptoms persist, take the bird to the vets for advice. There is no such thing as being over cautious.

Mutes:
Mutes should be white chalky liquid with a black centre. Green mutes sometimes occur when the bird is being dropped down to flying weight, because green suggests there is a low food intake. Notice if there is an offensive smell to the mutes, that too, suggests internal problems. Diarrhoea is normally an infection or lack of roughage, and tests should be done immediately. The same goes for traces of blood, which are usually a sign of worms. All raptors should be de-wormed two or three times a year.

Castings:
Castings will vary according to what the bird has eaten, for obvious reasons – the casting is the actual creature it digested. An unhealthy bird will produce castings that are irregular in shape and may contain undigested food. But undigested food can be a sign of gluttony, too, particularly during the moult when the diet could be more rich than the bird is used to. Occasionally problems could arise during the hunting season if the bird has been fed up on what it has killed. See frounce – listed below.

Other concerns are lack of appetite. Also watch out for a discharge from the eyes.

Respiratory Problems:
Respiratory problems are laboured breathing and wheezing, usually caused by dirty housing and poor ventilation. Asper is a fungal infection of the respiratory

tract, and can be followed by pneumonia. Both must be treated with antibiotics from your vet. Those antibiotics are usually Enrofloxacin, Amoxycillin-clavulanate and Oxytetracycline.

Frounce:

I sadly lost a Bengal Eagle Owl to frounce, caught from an infected pigeon. It is a horrible disease that creates cheesy plaque inside the mouth and growths on the tongue. The bird finds it very difficult to eat because of swelling inside the throat, and it is usually easy for a falconer to pick up on. It isn't a death sentence, but it must be treated by a vet in the early stages. Difficulty in eating can also be a cause of cuts in the mouth when a bird eats a bone that is too sharp. Infection can develop from this.

Sour Crop:

Sour Crop is easy to spot, a bulging crop (that hasn't digested) and sour breath. Its development can be brought on if the bird is taking antibiotics for another ailment. But usually it is a thin or weak bird gorging to the point of over-feeding. A vet will need to flush out the contents of the crop, usually under anaesthetic.

External Problems:

External problems caused because of hunting are normally more common than illness. Scratches and scrapes from barbed wire and brambles can be treated with Dermisol cream. Punctures and bites from squirrels and other raptors should be seen by an experienced vet.

Bumblefoot:

The feet are the only weapons your bird has to provide food, so any serious injury or infection is nothing short of a disaster to a bird of prey. Bumblefoot starts with a small corn on the base of the foot, then grows so painful that the bird will try and lie down rather than stand. It is caused by dirty perches, but those that feel that astroturf is superior to normal wood branches may be surprised to read that astroturf is supposedly one of the main causes. So, make sure all perches are cleaned regularly, wood or otherwise.

There is no cream or ointment that will miraculously take it away, so the corn has to be surgically removed. I wouldn't say it is anything that a regular vet couldn't perform, but the bird will need time out from hunting until the foot heals. I always advise cleaning the feet with antiseptic soap on a toothbrush. Get the bird used to the toothbrush during manning, so it becomes part of daily life.

Cuts and bites to a raptor's feet are part of the hunting process. They happen. But it is the falconer's responsibility to make sure they are spotted and treated early.

CHAPTER THIRTEEN – THE FINAL WORD

My thoughts and experiences are wrapped up in this little handbook, with the hope that some of it (at least) was of use to you. I don't profess to be a connoisseur, an authority on the subject of falconry, or a rocket scientist. I'm just a working class guy trying to give a bit encouragement to a working class public. It is aimed at the beginner, and I've tried to introduce you to the sport with a scattering of knowledge and a dash of humour. The book has been therapeutic for me to write because I fear dementia is kicking in and, sadly, in the not too distant future I will be reading it to try and remember what I once knew. Let's hope I find it interesting.

From the start of the book I introduced you to my school chums, Paul, Peter and Barry who went hunting for a Kestrel without a name. A ten year old never thinks about what can go wrong, only what can go right, and three little words – YES WE CAN! If your ambitions don't scare you – they aren't big enough.

Sadly Paul is no longer with us, he died of throat cancer in 2016. I lost track of old Charlie Sinclair when I left the area in 1984, and I never found out his fate. That saddens me. He was a proud man and an off-the-wall whimsical character the world needs more of. He encouraged me through the early stages of falconry, teaching me what can be achieved with patience and dedication. Yet I never gave him the satisfying feeling you get when someone says you inspired them.

After Charlie was Philip Glasier. Born Southfields, South-West London December 22nd 1915, he died September 11th 2000 aged 84.

I'm not saying a book can teach you the sum total, but a good book can motivate, which is equally important. I would like to mention an author who's falconry instruction and experience rose above the rest, with books that helped me achieve what I still do today. Glasier wrote in a simple language that was neither patronising nor did he try and portray that he was talking to the converted. I couldn't relate to any of it, but it infused in me what I wanted out of life. His publication 'As The Falcon Her Bells', produced in 1963, was the first book I ever bought with my own pocket money. I still have it today, weather-worn, dog-eared with passages highlighted in fluorescent ink. It taught me a lot, but mainly that life begins at the end of your own comfort zone.

He founded the Falconry Centre at Newent, Gloucestershire in 1967, then retired to Scotland in 1982. I went to the Centre many times but, sadly, never met the man.

One gentleman described him on a falconry forum: "I'm sitting here smiling to myself and thinking of the last time I visited Philip G when he said there were many aspects of falconry that had developed since opening the Falconry Centre that made him wish he hadn't. Philip was an irascible old sod, multi-talented, charismatic and quite brilliant, and I love him. He didn't suffer fools gladly."

One of the benefits of being a well-educated man is that you're not afraid of expletives, and you have no fear to put a fool in his place. That is the power of language and experience.

Happy flying.

Kev Fletcher.

THANKS

A special thanks to all who have been involved in the writing of this book, especially Jan Yarrow for her patience and support; Steve Mcdermott for the additional photographs; Chris Hocking for so many happy memories flying our birds; and Andy for letting me fly my birds at Rockliffe Hall Golf course.
A special mention to Amazon and Kindle, of course, for publishing the book.

MORE BOOKS FROM THIS AUTHOR –
Kev Fletcher

"The Durham Toll House"
"Visitor From The Somme"
"The Secret Gospel Of Holy Island"
"Beer, Bands & Bingo Balls"
All available on Kindle or from Amazon

ORIGINAL FALCONRY ARTWORK AVAILABLE

CONTACT Kev Fletcher:
kevfootymad@gmail.com